Alone feels like
Loneliness a___

"Overflowing with affection and humanity even as it examines difficult subjects, *The Loneliness Files* is one of those all-too-rare treats: a memoir to converse with. It is musical, truthful, and as I read, I left notes in the margins, re-examined my own experience of the global pandemic, and let the conversation re-shape my present. This book is a true gem, and only a superior essayist could have created it. Instead of putting it down when I finished, I flipped right back to page one and started over."

—ALEX JENNINGS,
author of *The Ballad of Perilous Graves*

"Haunting, affecting, and searingly smart, Athena Dixon's *The Loneliness Files* is both a mirror and soundtrack for our times. She offers us, in prose both lyrical and hypnotic, insights so unflinching they left me breathless. This book goes beyond one woman's loneliness to illuminate essential truths about our collective aloneness."

—JEANNINE OUELLETTE,
author of *The Part That Burns*

"In *The Loneliness Files*, Athena Dixon dissects the social constructs that both create and pathologize loneliness, ultimately concluding that the remedy might not be its eradication, but a radical re-envisioning of what loneliness can make possible: a deeper understanding of oneself, a deeper appreciation of the connections that keep us tethered to the world, and the absolute wonder of finding unexpected pockets of joy in solitude. Dixon writes with the astute candor of a recluse who has invited you into her most intimate spaces, ones that are rich with the minutiae of a contemporary life, and in so doing, she compels you to consider the intricacies of your own."

—DESTINY O. BIRDSONG,
author of *Nobody's Magic*

"Athena Dixon is my favorite sort of writer: Startlingly direct, vulnerable, and astonishingly honest. In *The Loneliness Files*, Dixon invites us to sit on her sofa with her, and with unflinching humility, reveals to us that her fear of dying alone is only eclipsed by her fear of not being remembered. I can assure you that anyone who reads *The Loneliness Files* will not be able to forget Dixon or her extraordinarily relatable journey."

—LAURA CATHCART ROBBINS,
author of the bestselling memoir,
Stash: My Life in Hiding

The
Loneliness
Files

The Loneliness Files

a memoir in essays

Athena Dixon

TIN HOUSE / PORTLAND, OREGON

Copyright © 2023 by Athena Dixon

First US Edition 2023
Printed in the United States of America

Manufacturing by Sheridan
Interior design by Beth Steidle

Library of Congress Cataloging-in-Publication Data

Names: Dixon, Athena, 1978– author.
Title: The loneliness files : a memoir in essays / Athena Dixon.
Description: First US edition. | Portland, Oregon : Tin House, [2023]
Identifiers: LCCN 2023025050 | ISBN 9781959030126 (paperback) |
ISBN 9781959030201 (ebook)
Subjects: LCSH: Dixon, Athena, 1978- | Social isolation. | Loneliness. |
Personal relations.
Classification: LCC HM1131 .D59 2023 | DDC 302.5/45—dc23/eng/20230605
LC record available at https://lccn.loc.gov/2023025050

Tin House
2617 NW Thurman Street, Portland, OR 97210
www.tinhouse.com

Distributed by W. W. Norton & Company
1   2   3   4   5   6   7   8   9   0

For
Willie Mae Horne, Timothann Horne, Norma
Jean Snow, Arielle Biggums, Tullis White,
Linda Krepps, and Michael Krepps

"For now she need not think about anybody. She could be herself, by herself. And that was what now she often felt the need of—to think; well, not even to think. To be silent; to be alone. All the being and the doing, expansive, glittering, vocal, evaporated; and one shrunk, with a sense of solemnity, to being oneself, a wedge-shaped core of darkness, something invisible to others. Although she continued to knit, and sat upright, it was thus that she felt herself; and this self having shed its attachments was free for the strangest adventures."

—VIRGINIA WOOLF,
To the Lighthouse

Contents

Part Three
Coming Home

Ephemera

The
Loneliness
Files

PART ONE
Life as It Is

RECOMMENDED LISTENING

"Blue Mesas" by Leon Bridges

"rises the moon" by Liana Flores

"Strange" by Celeste

Say You Will
Remember Me

remember loneliness because it is pervasive. It has a way of wrapping itself around me until it hides what's actually true. It squeezes tightly in my mind until what makes sense, what's actually happened, is distorted. Sometimes the loneliness makes me forget the goodness and the connection of my life. I find ways to compartmentalize these experiences until it is easy to remember only what I want. I think alone is sexy. Mysterious in its heaviness. Alone seems like a choice. Loneliness doesn't. This seems like I've been forgotten, passed over, discarded. It can feel like the world is way too bright—just an expanse of whiteness with nothing else in sight. It makes me feel singular and small.

On the cusp of 2021, in a green dress and red lipstick, I told myself I could cry. One wailing, sobbing mess of a breakdown between sips of liquor because when I woke up the next morning the world would appear to be new. This New Year's Eve was only a celebration of a year that needed to end. A year that saw some of us sink into isolation and others delve further into individualism and selfishness. This night was a cap to months of loneliness. A small bit of joy and release before heading into the bleakness of what seemed to be the coming year.

I'd checked out of the news months ago—too overwhelmed by death and discord that I felt myself slipping too much into darkness. This cry was a promise to myself that it would wash away the concrete deaths and dying dreams of what 2020 could have been. I had a book on the way and I'd finally started to find my voice when I'd been so sure I'd lost it. As selfish as my feelings may have been, it just wasn't fair and I wanted to wallow. I cried and then danced until my body slowed to rocking, and when the countdown ended the loneliness came in like a wave.

MY LONELINESS IS NOT GROUNDBREAKING, though. And it is not tragic. It just is. Nothing more and nothing less. I don't expect it to be important to anyone other than myself, but I write about it anyway. I turn it over like something precious in my hands—carefully as it floats across my fingers so I can see the details of it. Where dust and dirt and grit hide—the things that irritate and choke me when I breathe too deeply.

My loneliness is deep. It's oddly comforting because I know what to expect. It's like a light switch—sudden and complete—when it rears its head. My body starts to wind down and my mind disengages. Loneliness and isolation have been a slow build of contentment over the years before the sudden revelation of how the two are really disconnect disguised as choice. How between parents, a sibling, family, and friends is always the fear that I will die alone. That no one will remember me.

• • • • •

SOMETIME BEFORE CHRISTMAS IN 2003, London was headed toward the new year when Joyce Carol Vincent died

4

in front of the television. She wasn't found until January 2006. At the time of her passing she was 38. I had just turned 25. A set of coveted ages right in the middle of all the world is made for. I can only imagine we were a marketer's dream. When we think of the world, youth and beauty are at the center of it all. As time moves forward, the distance between importance and ourselves grows wider, though. But in the waning days of 2003, Joyce and I were insulated in my youth and her beauty— important if only for those reasons.

Joyce and I were an ocean apart, the bookends of Gen X. This generation of latchkey kids who knew how to survive alone. Years later, they'd call us the Forgotten Generation sandwiched between Boomers and Millennials and far removed from Gen Z. Joyce and I had hurtled past the start of the millennium and emerged into a world that was falling apart and coming together at the same time. War and terrorism and the heightening of the world's fears made an odd mix in a cloud of cyber connection. The planet was continuously in contact, yet somehow it was splintering at the seams.

2003 saw the start of the National Do Not Call Registry— another way to control access and ensure the links between us were ones we actually desired. The website 4chan began its path, and wars between the RIAA and music downloaders took to court. Between our emails and chatrooms and endless news cycles we saw everything, but we continued drifting into a world that seemed to only care about age/sex/location.

I wonder about the growing pile of electronic connections Joyce missed. Perhaps there was an extended away message on AIM or an inbox piling upon itself with spam. Had she started a MySpace during its first wave only for it to be abandoned without warning? Present day, these social threads seem so commonplace, but now how long would it take for red flags to raise? How long would her usernames have to remain dormant before someone thought to make physical contact? Without the constant expectation of likes and responses, just how much longer could she have lingered away from the fray even without her death?

· · · · ·

WHEN I READ ARTICLES ABOUT JOYCE, I noted how when the news broke there was no picture of her. She was simply an oddity dissolving quickly into a whisper. The public felt sorry for her until they determined there was a horrible reason for the disconnect. Carol Morley, a writer who took interest in Joyce's story, said in a 2011 article with the *Guardian*, "I watched as people discussed her in internet chatrooms, wondering if she was an urban myth, or talking about her like she never existed, calling her a couch potato, and posting comments such as: 'What's really sad is no one noticed she was missing—must have been one miserable bitch.'"[1] These people speculated on laziness, a deficient personality, or anything else to strip sympathy from her memory. I was sad when I read those articles and watched the videos on YouTube because I could see the opening of that path before me. What would the world say about me? How long would it take before I too am broken down to the parts of the story that draws the most clicks or views?

· · · · ·

WHEN MY BUILDING SUPER and an exterminator knock on my door one day, to make up for my missed appointment

---

1 https://www.theguardian.com/film/2011/oct/09/joyce-vincent-death-mystery-documentary.

from the month before, I feel there is more to their visit. The exterminator asks, "Is everything okay in here?" while his eyes sweep across the art and open space of my apartment. I think he believes I am a hoarder. Too many packages in and too few trips out, according to a neighbor I see near the dumpsters one day. I wish I would have said his perception of me is nothing more than simple consumerism—filling the void of depression with a brief jolt of materialistic serotonin. Sometimes my home echoes, and I am doing my best to manage this both physically and emotionally.

In the built-in dining room shelves there are rows and rows of colorful Fiesta teacups and matching saucers. Replacements of my favorite childhood toys and art prints I'm still buying frames for. I get package after package of vintage leather Coach purses, which I add to the shelves in the bedroom, and books that spill from cases in three rooms, a basket next to my sofa, and the storage space beneath it. I bring in clinking bags of candles that make my home smell like linen, lavender, and Nag Champa. There is the Black Americana that makes occasional visitors ask about the cast-iron water fountain signs and why I want to surround myself with these types of reminders.

Later that evening, the loneliness is a weight that affixes my body to the sofa—my mind knows I must move but is unable to gather my limbs. There is a sadness swimming beneath this feeling. It is more than exhaustion amid the endless global isolation ahead and behind. When the world opens again, in whatever form that may be, I am unsure I will be able to get out from under it. I've trained myself to think I am always okay with these feelings. I know that I am not, but it is how I survive when long stretches of time pass and I feel too needy to reach out to the world lest I come across as too much to bear.

• • • • •

NEARLY FIFTEEN YEARS AFTER they found Joyce's body, I have spent over a year in isolation—behind a mask and lacking human touch. I think I forget what it feels like to have another's skin against mine or the warmth of breath ghosting past my face. I am fearful I never will again. The disconnect of this is not the same, though. The absence of choice is the difference. Normally, I can determine when I am ready to deal with humanity and all it brings. Or when I want to leave or when I've reached my fill of interaction. But there is some isolation that grows outside of choice—fed by depression and sometimes unidentified fears. When I tell a friend I am writing about Joyce, and how I find a common link between us, he says that her isolation was by choice because it is easier to isolate than face the world. I can understand this.

People who knew her spoke highly of Joyce. Beauty. Talent. Charisma. Joyce was upwardly mobile—beautiful and successful in a world that holds these things like a prize. Until she slipped away. No one understands just how she came to be a near recluse who'd quit her job and died alone with a scattering of Christmas gifts beside her. I do. I think she'd learned to adapt to her loneliness and how it can creep up into everyday life. Perhaps she didn't want to become a burden when she felt the weight of it settling in.

I can't speculate on just what happened in Joyce's life that led to this solitary end, but I do know I recognize some of the signs. Pulling back from those who love you. Quitting. Hiding. Smiling and nodding so most interactions never go deeper than surface level. I know it is easier to appear to be what everyone expects than to show them who you truly are. What you really feel. The truth can be heavier than your burdens so you keep carrying them.

It is not hard for me to imagine the flicker of the television in front of her eyes. Or how she would have carefully balanced what she needed to wrap the gifts, piling the tape and scissors and paper beside her on the sofa. I can look to my right and see the detritus of life at my hip—holding the space where a person should be. When she was found, it was only through comparing her smile in a holiday photo to her dental records that led to her identification. It seemed a lonely end she did little to fight. Her life, no matter what of it was understood, moved unflinchingly forward around her no matter how much she had let go. It's just no one really noticed when her grip unfurled.

The world kept moving as Joyce's body wilted above the bustle of the Sky City Shopping Center situated below her home. The smell of her decomposition was attributed to the dumpsters lining a portion of the mall area in the space below, and it's reported a neighbor may have knocked due to the volume of her television. However, by the time she was discovered it was impossible to truly tell what caused her demise—her body had long since transitioned to the universe. Melted into the carpet, according to one of those who worked the scene.

In that article from the *Guardian*, the one by Carol Morley, the writer finds her way to Joyce's home. She takes in the energy around Sky City, trailing it as it tapers off until she reaches the green door behind which Joyce dwelled. She knocks, but no one answers. Morley asked the same questions I am, trying to understand how this death came to be by turning over the facts of Joyce's life. It seems a fool's wish to think we can find the heart of it there. I can't imagine there was anything left behind that can unravel the mystery all these years later. At best, we can take the bits we do know and determine if perhaps we are on the same path.

Imagine the black cabs dissecting the city of London, some of them having been papered with the question Morley sent across the city, *Do you know Joyce Vincent?* Imagine the newspaper ads among the classifieds too. I think of the concept of sonder. How bodies moved in and out of those cabs over days and months. What ads had been circled around the borders of that question. Did people try to answer as they traveled to and from their own lives? Did a few of them touch a spark of memory and make a call only to hear their Joyce pick up the phone? Or was Joyce just another entity in the world? Not important enough to be missed until it was far too late? Had she moved in the backgrounds of others' lives without ever being truly noticed? I am someone in the background of a picture. A blur in the street. A voice in the din of the world. Maybe there is the tiny remembrance of me in someone's history.

This is sonder—people sometimes so focused on their lives that the rest of us don't matter. We miss the interconnections. How we loop and lap each other never knowing what trails the person we've passed or just what awaits them once they are beyond our view. Joyce's life was a series of connections that should have rung the alarm. She was behind on rent during the months leading up to her discovery, and her utilities remained connected courtesy of automatic debits and debt-forgiveness programs. Joyce teetered above a safety net rife with holes large enough for her body to slip through. Joyce was known, but it was of no consequence. It was only when the business of the world could no longer exist around her absence that it truly mattered.

I wish there was another way to think of *known*. Maybe touched. I often remark to a friend, the same one who believes Joyce chose isolation, that I am always trying to place hands on him. Just to know he is alive and okay. Just to know that there is still a thread between us. We are mature enough to understand there may be stretches of time when it's just not possible to stay parallel. But even with my best efforts I once lost him for a year—the undertow of our lives was too powerful to keep either of us above the surface. Maybe the undertows rippling out from Joyce's loved ones made it too hard for them to find each other in the current, and by the time they floated back her way it was too late.

I've cultivated disconnect like Joyce—still the person everyone knows but with a hollowing inside. There must be some jettisoning to settle into being alone. There must be some fear. Some understanding that when the time comes no one will know. I try talking to people about this. I wonder openly about what will happen to me, without a spouse or children and hours from my family, as time continues to break down my body. I fret about how anyone will know that behind my triple-locked door I am suffering or gone. I speak lightly about home health aides and nursing homes because I am not sure just how far this loneliness will stretch. At the moment, I think it is forever. There is an overwhelming desire to plan for when I can no longer care for myself because I don't want to die alone.

I wonder if someone thought of Joyce during the three years her body sat in the glow of the television. Did someone call, but she was no longer there to answer? Did someone drive the block and look toward a window they thought to be hers? I would like to think so. I would like to think that in the sonder of our individual lives there are always quick glances beyond our own veils. It feels so much better to think of the world this way—sputtering connections that can sometimes charge to life and light our ways back to each other.

If I believe this, that sometimes drifting away from the world is not abandonment or isolation, it makes my own disconnect less frightening. It leaves me with hope that even if I am still sequestered in my own bedsit, it is not because I am forgotten. It is because life deems it so. Those connective threads, taut or slack between us, extend between everything and everyone. I think it takes time for us to realize in which direction life is pulling us and whether that is further away or closer to those we love.

Ghosts in the Machine

hortly after Joyce Carol Vincent began to swirl in my brain and I decided I wanted to explore what it means to be lonely, Elisa Lam came back into my orbit. I hadn't known much about her, just the startling video of her frightened or distressed in the Cecil Hotel elevator and the eventual gruesome knowledge of her death. Elisa was a perfect storm for the times we live in. She set out toward the bright lights of Los Angeles in the hopes of finding another piece of herself, but she never came back. She left a cloud of blog posts and photographs, as most of us do, never expecting them to come to a lingering end after her scheduled posts ran their course. She became infamous—some sort of beacon in the niche world of true crime and amateur sleuths.

Between YouTube videos analyzing the unsettling elevator tape and speculations on her death, she has existed as a mystery. Elisa has never been a person to most of the world it seems. She had those who loved her as we all do. Those who mourned her and deserve grace away from what the story has become. But as I dig deeper, it feels like she is only a case study for those looking for answers in shadows and a measure of notoriety. Perhaps we are all looking for a bit of fame, or infamy. Some of us find it without effort, whether that be good or bad, and others lose everything in its pursuit. Sometimes we are nothing but a proxy to someone else's story.

Months of disappearing into the murkiness of true-crime podcasts and eerie missing-person videos about Elisa and others has only scared me and pulled me deeper into feeling disconnected. These episodes have taught me, in some ways, to detach myself from the humanity behind the details. If you distill a person to a handful of salacious bullet points and a gruesome demise, you have what you need to forget they were an actual person. Instead, they are clips of audio, video, and cell-tower pings to analyze. If you are forced to remember anything other than this, that means you must see all a person contains. Maybe why we gravitate toward this type of entertainment is because it offers an outside view of the mundane and lets us believe that everything we do is actually important—we may just never know it.

On January 29, 2013, Elisa wrote on her blog, "I have arrived in Laland . . . / and there is a monstrosity of a building next to the place I'm staying / when I say monstrosity mind you I'm saying as in gaudy / but then again it was built in 1928 hence the art deco theme so yes it IS classy but then since it's LA it went on crack / Fairly certain this is where Baz Lurhmann needs to film the Great Gatsby." A monstrosity of a building. A monstrosity. A monster. One, that in all its gaudy beauty, sucked in lives and lore no matter how many times it has been, and will be, rebranded and scrubbed clean.

What I know of Elisa is the flash of her red sweatshirt and the stilted movement of her body in grainy surveillance video. I know the other guests complained of foul-tasting water and I know it was her body found floating in the water storage tank perched on the hotel's roof. How she came to be there, by fear or by freedom, has been determined to be an accidental drowning stemming from her bipolar diagnosis. But all she was before the elevator tape, and the discovery of her body, doesn't seem to matter to the story. With our growing infatuation with true crime, it is no small wonder her humanity is compartmentalized and reduced. I suppose this coincides with a need to transition people into content. It is much better to hinge experiences on anything except the mundane tragedy life can be. People die. And as trite as that may sound, sometimes that's all it is. It doesn't make the death less potent; it makes it more realistic.

It is widely accepted that the Cecil Hotel is haunted. When it opened in December 1924 things seemed normal. The seven hundred–room hotel rose among the other buildings in downtown LA—offering a clean bed at a fair rate. The lobby was something to behold, and years later the video of Elisa in the elevator and the hotel's dark history would serve as one of the inspirations for the *Hotel* season of the television series *American Horror Story*. The season partially inspired by the Cecil Hotel played into the death and murder and ruin of it, showing souls trapped in an endless loop never to escape the hotel's clutches. Elisa was not one of the ghosts, but in the real world so much of the true-crime coverage of her passing has trapped her there anyway.

Or perhaps the Cecil Hotel is cursed, depending on which version of the history you believe. Maybe the hotel's true tragedy is not the souls left in limbo within its walls but instead something that draws bad energy and killers to this place. The hotel has most certainly had more than its fair share of tragedy, and that tragedy makes anything that happens on these grounds a mystery even if they are sadly nothing more than an average person leaving their loved ones to grieve their loss. There is always a need for more here. To this end, Elisa has become an urban legend or some kind of thrill for people to chase down hallways and up to the rooftop overlooking LA. I can't help but think her being an urban legend makes her an even lonelier figure. I worry Elisa is now just a symbol, not a soul.

In February 2021, eight years after her death, Netflix launched a series about Elisa's disappearance at the hotel. I binge watch it in one morning while I am supposed to be working. Hunched over my laptop, I stop after each episode and take notes because a voice actress reads portions of Elisa's Tumblr. Her words resonate with me because their probing of the world around her makes sense to a person still struggling to put *that* world into focus. Who we are and how we become those people in relation to everything around us is at the core of how I start to believe Elisa and I are connected.

I find common ground with her because I often feel the victim of my own haunting. I once wrote that I felt like a ghost in a machine. That I was putting everything in my heart onto the keyboard in front of me and hoping someone, anyone, would reach back and understand. Elisa wrote on her blog, Nouvelle-Nouveau, "I suppose that is the human condition / to feel so big, so important / but at the same time / be just a flicker in the universe / and the struggle to come to terms with those two truths."[2] The truth was, and still is, I am trapped too.

---

2 https://nouvelle-nouveau.tumblr.com/post/36405058999.

Trapped in the same loop of trying to understand my place in the world. Trapped by lingering bad decisions and future fears.

Elisa's blog brings me to sonder. John Koenig coined the word in 2012 in his work *The Dictionary of Obscure Sorrows*. This new word makes sense to me. He writes,

> The realization that each random passerby is living a life as vivid and complex as your own—populated with their own ambitions, friends, routines, worries and inherited craziness—an epic story that continues invisibly around you like an anthill sprawling deep underground, with elaborate passageways to thousands of other lives that you'll never know existed, in which you might appear only once, as an extra sipping coffee in the background, as a blur of traffic passing on the highway, as a lighted window at dusk.[3]

Sonder is the universe unraveling from the top all the way down to our individual lives. But under scrutiny, or simply a longer gaze, we see it's all made up of fibers entangling to make something stronger—a binding to pull together each piece of us collectively. What we can hope for is that someone sees us in the short time we are illuminated. But that's the fear, to have a split second of brightness and extinguishing before we are ever truly known.

I'm almost afraid to scroll Elisa's Tumblr. It is a bit frightening it is still there after her passing, but digital death isn't the same as the death of flesh. Ghost profiles and queues trick us into believing there is always someone there just waiting

---

3 John Koenig, *The Dictionary of Obscure Sorrows* (New York: Simon & Schuster, 2021).

behind the cursor. One of my Tumblr friends died five years ago. When I search the archives of my account I see the GoFundMe posts for her homegoing service reblogged time and again by mutuals, but her page looks as if she is still among the living. Her last post is bittersweet—a pink box, black letters saying "Page 365 of 365."

I think if I find my way to Elisa's page, I am disturbing something. Perhaps I feel as if I would be gawking at her demise, but our shared loneliness makes me believe there is something there I may need. I point the browser to the correct spot and am greeted by a white page. I think I've stumbled into a trap, some sick internet joke just waiting for a jump scare, but her words and images are simply hidden in the archives. The queue has run out.

I am not sure what I am hoping to find there. Perhaps there is something kindred—posts, photos, or anything else that links us. Maybe we reblogged the same beautiful aesthetics or quotations over pastel backgrounds. Connection is the crux of it. I'm always seeking it even if it frightens me to think that one day someone may actually want to touch me and see if I am solid. I feel like smoke and I can't help from thinking Elisa did too. Smoke tells you something is burning, but it is the intention of the flame that matters. We are either warming or we are destroying. I'm not always quite sure which one applies.

I enter the archives of the site and stare at the minimalist pages for a measure then close my laptop before deciding to continue my exploration the next morning. The brightness of day is much better. In the light, I can fight the sadness and obsession I know will come from wading through this digital diary. It's part rubbernecking—trying to determine if there was a way her death could have been predicted or if there's more of me in her actions than I am too uncomfortable to admit. Daytime connects me to responsibilities and expectations. The hours are not really my time to own.

When I venture back the next morning, I am on edge, hoping to find something profound. One of the talking heads in the documentary says we were cheated out of a brilliant writer in the making. I prepare to feel inadequate because this woman, even in her death, is supposed to be the writer I wish I could be. I am comforted and I am happy with what I find.

I find her. I find me. What I see in her words is a push toward the hope of understanding how the pieces of her brain and the world fit together. If they do, in fact. There is something kindred between me and Elisa. A wanderlust that compels the two of us to pack our bags and see what life has to offer under a new sky. I latch on to the posts leading up to her fatal trip— remembering how many times I've struck out on my own and how there was always a taste of worry laced beneath the excitement. I think it's the edge of fear, or the edge of danger, that makes me feel like I'm alive. In my twenties it was nothing for me to drive around a city until I was lost deep in the belly of it and polled strangers on which way to go. I believed in the fundamental goodness of people. My best friend calls my attitude Midwest friendly—polite and likely way too trusting at the offset.

On her Tumblr, Elisa muses about what her life is, what it could be, what she wants it to be. She chooses things for her posts that spark her interest—beautiful words and images balanced with the singe of darkness at the edges. I think the darkness isn't always troubling. It's just the spaces at the edges of things still passed over by the light. What we do in those liminal spaces can be the problem.

In February 2013, the month of her death, Elisa (or her blog's queue) posted a sketch by Justine Frank. This 1927 piece, from a series titled *The Stained Portfolio*, is a quadrant of a female profile morphing and distorting from a visage easily recognized to a void with tendrils exploding from a center mass. The same year Frank created the series, the first suicide was recorded at the Cecil Hotel. A man, distraught over family issues, shot himself in the head. Other suicides followed over the next decades, including one via poison capsules in 1931, until an unlucky thirteen of them were logged at final count according to Wikipedia. The rooms and hallways trapped people in all strides of life—those broken and looking for repair; those unwilling to gather the pieces of their lives; and those wanting to shatter anything they touched.

It is, of course, easy to ruminate on how these sketches, and even those other deaths, mimic Elisa's lonely end. Perhaps in these years after her passing, the changed profile sketched by Justine Frank is more about what we have all become collectively and the gray spaces we now occupy. These liminal spaces are transitions between two states of being. Between what we are and what we wish to be. Or where we've been and where we are going. I think they expand or contract with our lives. Sometimes these spaces seem as vast as fields stretching out green into the horizon while others only slip into space before everything we thought we'd known is now behind us. Maybe if we latch on to life, too much in anticipation of the future or too much in the past, we upset the balance of who we are supposed to be.

These liminal spaces are the fine lines we walk toward something new, but it doesn't mean we can't move backward. I can't help but to believe these spaces are now digital—a nebulous haze of connection that can be nothing more than smoke—the same kinds in which Elisa was lost. Spaces in which we believe that there are no negative trade-offs in the expansions of our worlds. Where the last frantic moments of a woman's life can be tied to paranormal elevator games or pinned on an innocent man whose life is ruined in the "solving" of the crime. The liminal spaces of our new world are massive—easy for us to be swallowed into—and disorienting. We can only hope we are headed in the right direction when we enter and come out on the other side still whole.

Said the Spider
to the Fly

"Will you walk into my parlour?" said the Spider to the Fly,
"'Tis the prettiest little parlour that ever you did spy;
The way into my parlour is up a winding stair,
And I have many curious things to shew when you are there."
"Oh no, no," said the little Fly, "to ask me is in vain,
For who goes up your winding stair can ne'er come down again."[4]

eneva Chambers was, by all accounts, mean. I struggled writing that sentence. As simple as it may be, what it does is distill an entire life into a singular, flat character judgment. Whatever dimension that existed in her life is pulled away. She is now whatever the word "mean" represents for the person saying it. They remember the elementary school bully. An abrasive teacher. A hated coworker. An ex-lover or friend. "Mean" colors how a person is remembered. Determines what kind of respect we put on their name or how seriously we take what's become of them.

---

4 https://www.poetrybyheart.org.uk/poems/the-spider-and-the-fly/.

"Mean" is judge, jury, and executioner. There is no way around the label—really no way out of it other than some worse character trait attached to someone else. Sometimes "mean" is a way we can divert the spotlight from our own share of the blame and make ourselves clean. I wrote that Geneva was mean because that is how the world was introduced to her.

After I heard about Geneva Chambers for the first time, I dropped her name into Google and came away with so few results that I thought perhaps I was spelling it incorrectly or I'd somehow missed the follow-ups after the news broke. Geneva fascinated me. But it was not her death that held my interest. It was a woman, very much known to the world, who had made the decision to shut out everyone and keep living on her own terms.

I watched a couple of YouTube videos that used Geneva as one of a handful of stories about lonely corpses. One of those videos tells the story of a Croatian woman whose body sat in an apartment for forty-two years untouched. In the same video there is a mention of twins, Anthony and Andrew Johnson, who died side by side in recliners only to be discovered in 2014. They died in 2011. The compilation videos gave me only a surface-level view of Geneva, but she stuck with me so much that I've performed that search many times with the same results. I keep hoping some combination of words and quotation marks will lead me to something more.

Those scant articles and videos all said the same thing. Geneva was far from friendly. According to the stories, she wanted nothing to do with anyone. It seemed she'd distanced herself from family and she had no friends. Geneva played her gospel music and stuck to herself. She refused freshly baked cookies from one neighbor. She yelled at children. Those living near her had been put off by her yelling and just how abrasive she could be so they altered their lives in deference to her. They avoided walking on the sidewalk near her home. After she faded away from sight they started strolling past her house again. It was a brand new day. Almost like the scene in *The Wiz* when Evillene dies and the poor trapped souls are finally free.

When I searched Google, I was met with nothing about who she was outside of the circumstances of her death. It took about three years, or so investigators believe, from the time she died of cardiovascular disease and diabetes in her bed, to the time someone found her body. A landscaper noticed a patio door ajar and called the authorities. There Geneva was. No longer mean, just dead. Geneva can't defend herself now or explain why she behaved how she did. There is no family or any friends coming to sing her praises. Or at least I've yet to come across them. We know how Geneva refused to live by social graces and the niceties required to live in society. I believe she understood the expectation of a friendly wave or smile. That even silence is better than a raised voice because at least then there is some gray area about how you feel. I also think she didn't give a damn.

· · · · ·

AN ARTICLE ABOUT THE DISCOVERY of Geneva's body opens with a description of spider webs hanging from her red front door.[5] For years after she was last seen there were no lights inside her home and no signs of life. People simply thought she'd abandoned her home, and they kept her lawn in order out of those same social graces she shunned. I don't want to forget that this detail about Geneva exists nor do I want it to

_____
5 https://www.tampabay.com/news/publicsafety/body-found-inside-largo-home-identified/2136469.

get lost in the web of screenshots I use as a makeshift research document. I'm obsessed with these lonely ends. I keep running into stories about them and I can't let go because more often than not they are a reflection of me.

What sticks with me is the image of the spider webs in the corner of the door and what kind of barrier can be so delicate yet still so impossible to break. Imagine Geneva's neighbors attempting to communicate with her, trying to offer the most basic of human kindness. How her rebuffing must have felt like batting away invisible threads—the feel of them clinging afterward like a million tiny legs. Then Geneva, tucked away in her corner watching it all, disinterested and disgusted by their efforts.

I realize, just on the edge of sleep, that sadly unlike it appeared for Geneva, I am profoundly, openly, and enthusiastically loved. If there were to be an article about the discovery of my body, there would most certainly be cobwebs, but I think the stories told about me would be a bit more kind. I think its writer would say I was aloof but a good person. Nice but not friendly. That maybe I spent a little too much time alone. I think its writer would say this was by choice.

I want to understand how Geneva locked herself away. I give humanity to her decision because I understand that all of this "witch of the neighborhood" nonsense is likely the result of shyness or trauma or fear. How easy would it be for me to go the way of Geneva and shutter myself into a situation possibly too complicated to fix? I want to look away from the idea that it was just pure meanness that drove her to isolation. I like to believe that perhaps the world had been mean to Geneva and this was her way of coping—to hurt it before it hurt her.

Sometimes I have a layer of anger over what I feel, and even if a simple phone call or text can fix what's wrong, I can't bring myself to make the call or write the text. I say this is because I don't want to be the bigger person, and that is for the most part true. If I feel hurt or wronged, my feelings add to the general disconnection that is always present. These two in concert are sometimes impossible to overcome. Pride may be a part of this. I know that it is, but the malaise of at times self-induced loneliness is the real problem. Perhaps it is part trauma—from the fear of letting people get too close to me lest the terrible letdowns and pain I've felt circle back to buckle me once more. That's not true, though. Those heartbreaks came years later— decades after childhood and years before the current state of my life. This leaves me thinking if the silences I've wallowed in are truly only as lonely as I've made them.

· · · · ·

THE AUTHORITIES THINK GENEVA was dead for three years before they found her. If the condition of her body, and the last reports of when she was last seen were true, 2010 seems the likely year of her death. I think of how a part of me died over that span of time between when she died and when she was found too. How I shut out most of the world because that was the easier path than letting someone near me. In a scrap of essay tucked away on my laptop I tried to catalog what I owned in the apartment I hid in while wrapping my mind around the idea of remaining alive.

A bed/a couch/a dresser/a rocking chair/a valet chair/a red school chair/three suitcases of clothes/one suitcase of shoes/ two plastic totes of underwear, T-shirts and scarves/three coats/four purses/two boxes of household decorations/ thirty books and ten DVDs/six Bjork CDs/two cooking pots/two plates/six glasses/two coffee mugs/two spoons/

two forks/two knives/one skillet/one iced tea pitcher/ one slotted spoon/one spatula/one soup pot/one casserole dish/a tea kettle/four mixing bowls/four eating bowls/one salt shaker/one blue colander/one sheet set/one comforter/ two pillows/two laptops/one lamp/one candle/one shower curtain/a night light and a car all stored in two bedrooms/ four walk-in closets/one walk-in pantry/a large kitchen/a bathroom/a living room with a fireplace/a sun porch/a dining room/a basement/a driveway.

That home echoed. I lived in my bedroom. Listened to music on one of the laptops or my phone. Watched a DVD now and then. *Lost in Translation. Eternal Sunshine of the Spotless Mind. Like Water for Chocolate. Y Tu Mamá También. Amélie.* When I did eat, I made small meals in the kitchen and ate them on the edge of my bed, sometimes the couch. My fridge was nearly bare, as were the cupboards. I had not transferred my mail from my parents' home to my new address in order to limit the scope of my view. There were no rugs to dampen the sounds of my footsteps on the hardwood floors. I got dressed in the second bedroom under a single, bright ceiling light. I prepared for the day in the bathroom, willing myself to stitch together some semblance of a human face to show the world.

Life, the solitary one I cultivated by choice and by circumstance, was one of conscious effort. It was not due to lack of money, family, or friends. It wasn't for lack of love. I made that choice for the discomfort of it. To shrink down my emotions into something easily hidden—perhaps small enough to swallow whole. I was fanatical in my pursuit of that discomfort. I existed in the bare minimum. No television or cable. No internet save the hotspot I used via my phone when I needed contact with the outside world. I wanted to die then and I did everything I could to push away those who loved me and even those who didn't know me. It was obvious at the time I was loved and that I loved in return, but I stretched the distance between those relationships until the threads were so thin it was a wonder they didn't break.

One afternoon my father must have heard the drifting in my voice. I'd told him I was tired. Tired was the only word I could think of. It wasn't sadness. Wasn't anger. Wasn't rage. Wasn't heartbreak. I was tired. My dad took the few short blocks, which seemed a planet away, to that echoing apartment and brought me home. I left that catalog of things alone in that shell of a home until I was able to gather enough of the pieces of myself to take what I wanted and leave the rest. Even now, some of those things are still boxed in the basement of my parents' house—molding books, clippings from newspapers, scrapbooks, and photos of a life long gone. Eventually I will throw those out too.

If we were to step back from the blip of information about Geneva's life, perhaps we can see this same cataloged sadness. What was contained within the walls of her home? What was carted out when finally she was laid to rest? All we can do now is speculate if these same feelings of despair and apathy were the same for Geneva. What I know is that for a year after I signed the lease on that apartment, I did my very best to sink into some sort of oblivion. It didn't matter who may have loved me or how I was supposed to be connected to the world at large. Somewhere in the lonely end of Geneva's life I think she must have also felt the same way. I can relate to the sort of pain, or fear, that drove her so deeply into the shadows, and I believe I've come to know what it was for me. I wish there was a way to actually answer this question for her.

I am still here living, though, so it is possible to begin to explain what led me to that place. I could perhaps dig around in my brain and find an experience that proves the profound sense of loneliness I've always felt, but it is hard to put a spotlight on something that is as wide as the world in which it exists. Everything is illuminated, nothing is shadow. But I'm coming to believe my disconnection, or is it better to say difficulty connecting, isn't necessarily negative. It kind of just is. There are people I truly and deeply care about and who I want to keep in the insular group that matters most to me. Yet, even in those connections I feel there is still a distance. Be it physical or emotional, how I relate to people seems to be at an arm's length. It's hard to get around that.

I am overwhelmingly lonely. And I cannot believe that doesn't matter and I will not believe there are not scores of others like me. I know there are those who feel the world is always just a little too far away or a little too close—never comfortable in either situation. Those who would love to be a part of all life has to offer fully, but something just doesn't click. Those people who crave the smallest of touches but get lost in the fear of what could go wrong, not all that could be right.

●●●●●

I CAN'T CATALOG MY LIFE NOW. The things I own are far too vast for me to not tire typing and listing them. In some ways I've filled in those silent spaces with things that bring me joy. Bright blue sofas; colorful Fiesta teacups and teapots; Black Americana; art and books and records and plants and trinkets and bobbles. This is where I now rest. One night, amid my endless scrolling, I came across a video of a maximalist apartment. The woman in the voiceover said that she wanted to buy the things that made her happy and to have enough of an interesting life that the estate sale after her death would be cool. I think this is me now. I want to leave something behind no matter how secretive its curation may have been. My life has spiraled out of the isolation I was once so oddly proud of and become one of a different choice. I choose now to connect and know keenly when I must untether.

I've tried to lose this sense of untethering before, but it is important for me to share there is most certainly joy in my solitude. Those moments I feel the comforting weight of the life I've built settling in around me. When I can run my fingers over the items I've collected because they bring levity or curiosity. During a visit to one of my apartments, either in Ohio or Pennsylvania, my father entered and said, "It looks like you live here." And I do *live* here. In all the broken connections and tangled threads, I am living in the forefront and the sonder of each day. I have hope that if somehow I am swallowed beneath the surface of this life, someone would care. There would be a moment when my absence was felt and one of those who love me would come looking because I am living and touching everything around me.

A few years ago, when I first wrote about my loneliness, I was in the midst of a suicidal year full of isolation and depression, and I was far too damaged to share what I felt or seek help. That loneliness has morphed and, in some odd ways, grown. It is a part of me now. Kind of like the tiny boxer's cut on my right cheek. I don't remember how I got the scar, the memory is long faded, but it's there and some days it seems to dominate my view of my face. That's what this loneliness is, something I can hide with a few feathery brush strokes, but the ghost of the injury is still visible just below the paint.

What helps me hide this void are the connections I've made. Like one sleepy morning when I roused from bed in Berkeley, California, because my group chat with Marisol and Kym wouldn't stop pinging over and over again. How I threatened them with death if they texted another time because Philadelphia and Berkeley are hours apart and I was trying to sleep. And how they laughed like they knew those threats were the furthest thing from reality. Or how I knew when I returned from that writing jaunt we'd crowd around a bar or a breakroom table or one of our desks and laugh and laugh. That, finally, these two women had given me what I so desperately hope Geneva had—sets of extra arms reaching out.

• • • • •

IN JAPAN THERE IS a minister of loneliness. This person is tasked with addressing the growing problem of a rising suicide rate as well trying to reduce loneliness and isolation. There are about one million people in Japan who purposefully isolate themselves from the world. In 1998, Japanese psychiatrist Professor Tamaki Saito first defined "the term hikikomori (derived from the verb *hiki* 'to withdraw' and *komori* 'to be inside'). Saito chose the term to describe the many young people he saw who didn't fit criteria for mental health diagnosis, but were nonetheless in a state of extreme, distressing withdrawal."[6] But the *hikikomori* have existed well before the position of the minister of loneliness was created in 2021. I'd seen brief clips of stories of these people who seemed afraid to interact with the outside world. I am not in this

---

6 https://theconversation.com/hikikomori-understanding-the-people-who-choose-to-live-in-extreme-isolation-148482.

place. At least not yet, but I've pondered before just what it would take to push me over the edge into this type of abyss.

I believe this catalyst wouldn't be grand. I cannot imagine some great tragedy that would finally be the straw to push me inside, fearful and unwilling to come out. It will be something small. A day that all the energy has drained from my body and I can no longer pretend. A night when in the darkness I decide there is nothing better for me outside the doors of my home. When the scale of life reaches the tipping point, and I'm flung far away when the weight of it all comes crashing down.

Just like with the things that have fascinated and frightened me about the prospects I've been exploring, I begin to catalog what I know about these people—comparing and contrasting who I am with who they've been reported to be. Perhaps I am allowing myself too much grace when I say that because I have an occasional outing with friends and commute to an office three days a week the same feelings of the *hikikomori* do not live in my chest. But I know they do.

The Japanese Ministry of Health, Labor, and Welfare list the guidelines for *hikikomori* as follows:

1. a lifestyle centered at home;
2. no interest or willingness to attend school or work;
3. symptom duration of at least six months;
4. schizophrenia, mental retardation, or other mental disorders have been excluded; and
5. among those with no interest or willingness to attend school or work, those who maintain personal relationships (e.g., friendships) have been excluded.[7]

---

7 https://www.ncbi.nlm.nih.gov/pmc/articles/PMC4912003/.

Here is what I know about myself:

1. My entire life exists within a two-bedroom apartment in a city 378 miles away from my hometown. I have spent the vast majority of two years in that apartment alone with only the sound of my own voice and those piped into my computer via YouTube. The people I love exist only on screens during a time when the world is dying. This keeps us all safe, if not yearning for comfort. It will take a year plus one month from the first lockdown before I can hug my sister and see her eyes dancing just above a mask. I will not touch her again for another six months after that. That will be at the funeral of our cousin and the first in a string of deaths over the next year.

2. When coworkers ask me, virtually or now in person, how I am, I often answer "I am here." It means that I am here because I am obligated and I must make money to survive. It means that given the opportunity I would sit in silence in my living room and listen to the cars rush by on the streets below.

3. Seven years ago I moved to a city I barely knew to prove a point. I was strong and needed no one else. Each year that goes by I get more and more comfortable in the silences and the distance. This does not stop me from feeling guilty about that move.

4. An old therapist said what I was experiencing was depression. Said it was anxiety. Said it was adjustment disorder. My current therapist lets me ramble and asks pointed questions to bring me to new places I've yet to

explore about myself. I know she believes I am sane, but I still worry when she takes notes.

5. I have friends. I have family. I maintain those relationships the best I can, but I often feel selfish. I often feel outside of myself. I often feel I am not living up to what I need to be even if no one has ever asked me to be anything but myself.

When I flip through photos and videos of the *hikikomori* I pretend I do not see myself reflected in what I observe. I create distance between what I believe they are and who I am. But maybe what has been labeled my depression is more closely parallel to the life of the *hikikomori* than I am willing to admit or what has been diagnosed. So easily I can rationalize how I live—so quietly and hidden that those in the closest proximity seem to not know I am there. I exist—that is vastly true— but I feel like a ghost. Not fully fleshed but enough to draw attention when noticed. There is a rising term, *sotokomori*, that hopes to capture those not fully isolated who perhaps do their best existing online. Their withdrawal from society is still extreme by "normal" standards, but it is at least a bridge between a forced social life and being the alpha and omega of your own world.

I have spent a large majority of my adult life crafting exactly who I want to be in every username and profile I've built. I move between these identities without thinking as a sense of protection and as a measure of distance. I have found love and lust and friendships and enemies all from within the confines of my home and for the vast majority of those interactions I have been safe.

In some ways the idea of *sotokomori* suits me so much better than being a person in the "real" world. I sometimes make short video diaries on my Instagram account about rejection, imposter syndrome, jealousy, and joy. I talk into the camera because I am convinced even if there are only a handful of people who care, I am not alone. What I'm doing is keeping myself subtly connected to the world. Just a few blinking cursors away from a group of people who will understand.

I've arrived at this particular point of my life because I've chosen it. It was not by force of nature nor any other unwieldy thing beyond my grasp. It is because this is comfortable— requires so little effort outside of me that the momentum to get out of the slump is not there. "I have my life, I'm living it. It's twisted, exhausting, uncertain, and full of guilt, but nonetheless there's something there," writes Banana Yoshimoto in *The Lake*. In the echo of this living, there is peace just as much as fear. Just as much there is often too much quiet and too much space. I've begun to fill in the gaps, but there is still so far to go.

I should stand in what I've created and figure out just how much of it is some sort of self-fulfilling prophecy—a manifest destiny of loneliness. I know the truth of what I've been living in all its ugliness, all its shame, and all its damage. I know how history remembers the lonely. Some of us are footnotes and asterisks. Oddities to dissect against the scale of the social. A tally of friends and followers and digital impact. What is the legacy we each leave behind if not some lingering performance of how we lived? This is loneliness of another kind.

• • • • •

Said the cunning Spider to the Fly, "Dear friend, what can I do,
To prove the warm affection I've always felt for you?
I have, within my pantry, good store of all that's nice;
I'm sure you're very welcome —will you please to take a slice?"
"Oh no, no," said the little Fly, "kind sir, that cannot be,"
I've heard what's in your pantry, and I do not wish to see!"

In the ending of the article about Geneva, one of her neighbors wonders what kind of life she lived. "Very sad situation. A very lonely person . . . What kind of life did she have?" he questioned.[8]

I will fill in the gaps for Geneva. She was not *just* mean. She had a life that existed before any in the neighborhood ever knew her. I believe she was loved. Even if it was only by one person, decades in the past. There were things that made her laugh and things that brought her joy. Geneva created her own space—she did own her home prior to her death—and she filled it with the kind of existence she wanted or perhaps needed to navigate the world as she saw it in front of her.

Perhaps the best place to concentrate is on the why of all the "kindness" sent her way. After the lights stopped coming on in Geneva's house, how long did it take for someone to knock? Did someone knock at all? After the gospel music stopped playing and Geneva's door never opened and the grass grew longer and no groceries came in and no trash went out and the mail piled up, did any of the freshly baked cookies and friendly waves matter? Maybe Geneva was protecting herself—no longer the spider but now the fly—from the traps laid out before her.

---

8 https://www.tampabay.com/news/publicsafety/body-found-inside-largo-home-identified/2136469/.

There is a fine line between private and reclusive. One allows you the dignity to make decisions of your own accord under no one's eyes except your own. I think the other is a reaction to perceived danger—another offshoot of fight or flight. I suppose Geneva was well out of bounds—had far crossed over the line of being a recluse where no one could reach her. Maybe that is how she wanted it. Maybe that was what was necessary for her survival. But her disappearance from the neighborhood cannot simply be chalked up to her being a recluse. Be it morning, afternoon, or night, there are always eyes, and if people could make character judgments, they could most certainly recognize when the woman containing such a spirit was no longer there. That is the trap I believe Geneva may have been trying to avoid. I think she gave herself over to a social death rather than a personal one because it allowed her the dignity of which we now see she's been stripped.

The Ruin of
Rom-Coms

When I say to my therapist I feel like Teri from *Soul Food*, she knows exactly what I mean. I often sprinkle in pop culture when I try to explain how I feel in our sessions. Luckily, I never have to break down these references to her. Having a Black woman as a therapist is a gift hard to quantify. Before I found her, I'd been out of therapy for years since my last provider, Ann, retired. No one since had matched up to the comfort I felt with her. But this Blackness coupled with that comfort, and wrapped in just as much kindness and understanding, is new. These sessions are one of the only places I feel I can lay myself bare. I've cried from the moment my therapist has blinked onto the screen before. Slipped in jokes as a pressure valve and as a means of unfurling what I'm really feeling. Our weekly meetings are exercises in letting go in order to reconnect, maybe even learning for the first time, forgotten pieces of myself. These unpackings are how I begin each Saturday morning.

I tell my therapist during a session deep into the summer how lonely this phase of my life feels. No matter how close I am to finally achieving my dreams I am still unmoored. We chat about how I am craving the creature comforts of having a partner—that those pseudo relationships in my life are not as fulfilling as they used to be. A series of these half relationships have carried me for years, but right now in the thick of the August heat I want so badly to have someone to truly call my own.

During one session, I quote a few lyrics from the group Little Brother about the complexity of wanting someone to love when I don't want to be bothered most days. This is selfish, I suppose. I'm in that situation right now. Halfway in love with someone who it seems relates to the lyric as well. Far too many days I find myself holding my breath and waiting for the hot to burn more intensely than the cold that is beginning to show up way too often in our interactions.

I say to my therapist that I wish I could skip the first year in a relationship so I don't have to make getting-to-know you small talk. Or maybe because by then I'll know if my heart is safe. Or that I don't want a syrupy sweet love or daily good morning texts or to be touched all the time. I want someone there, supportive, in his own world, but still connected to mine. I don't think this is realistic, but the heart wants what it wants.

We've talked about me downloading the dating apps again and at least attempting to interact with the men who show interest. If I am actually serious about being in a relationship after many years alone, I cannot expect a man to come falling into my lap. Life is not a movie. There will be no "meet-cute" for me. No matchmaking best friend. No enemies turned lovers. No happenstance that turns to romance.

In most of the romance movies I've watched over the course of my lifetime, obstacles to love never seem to be an issue for long. Sure the woman may be a little nerdy or off-kilter in some way, but once she's given the appropriate makeover, or at least takes off her glasses, all of the obstacles to love are removed. Or sometimes the lead is the hot girl who's never been seen for who she is and when the male love interest comes stumbling into her life the skies open up. The movies I find myself most drawn to are the aspirational ones. Like *Love Jones*. I was still in high school when it debuted, but by the time my college years rolled around, the moody Chicago scenes were exactly what I thought I wanted and deserved.

I'd already crafted my life into the Ohio version of this movie—open mics, headwraps, jazz albums, local dive bars, and private house parties. Even now I look back at those times as some of the best of my life. Poor and uncertain as I may have been. It seemed only natural I'd find a relationship just like the one in the movie—staring out from the stage or shoulder to shoulder during some philosophical debate. It never happened. Instead, I've tripped and fallen into relationships out of desperation, fleeting sparks, or by cause of years not affection.

* * * * *

I TAKE MY THERAPIST'S ADVICE and download a couple of apps, and in one afternoon on Plenty of Fish I get twenty-five messages. I refuse to open any of them out of fear. On Tinder I rarely match with anyone because I find myself far too critical to swipe right. I overanalyze the profiles and pictures and usernames. Then I make snap decisions about why the men may not like me. The same is true for Hinge, OkCupid, Match, Black People Meet, and Bumble. This analysis is an extension of that fear. Of being known or having to show my flaws and hope they are still acceptable. Or to open myself to the possibility of yet another mismatch. Or even worse, being invisible altogether.

In a now deleted blog post, a cofounder of OkCupid reported that data showed "most men on the site rated black women as less attractive than women of other races and ethnicities. Similarly, Asian men fell at the bottom of the preference list for most women."[9] Where does that leave me? A Black woman. Older. Larger. Taller. None of these descriptors fall within the spectrum of what society has deemed conventionally attractive and desirable—those openly courted en masse in our media. Perhaps I am a walking red flag to the men behind the profiles. Maybe I am even that dreaded invisible. And this is why on those one-off occasions I actually read the previews or open a few messages fully, they are nothing except either completely banal or explicit. There is no middle ground in getting to know me, but I've learned this well, haven't I? I've been in this loop of download, try, and delete far too many times.

All of this leaves me out in the cold. The book *The Dating Divide* notes that "white daters are more likely to ignore overtures from people of color who hold a conventionally more desirable education background, height, and body type, while being responsive to those who lack those qualities, but are still white." Maybe, if I am lucky, I can become some sort of fetish or a quick roll around in the darkness. Studies like those in *The Dating Divide* serve no other purpose than making me believe women like me don't get chosen. This leaves me feeling so far

---

9 https://www.npr.org/2018/01/09/575352051/least-desirable-how-racial-discrimination-plays-out-in-online-dating.

flung from the center of desire that it's beginning to make little sense to even try.

At times we, these undesirables, can fall into the realm of the fetishized and not be seen as viable partners. Sometimes it seems we should be grateful for any attention at all. I've seen this firsthand. Once, when I paid to join one of the subscription dating sites, I took care in crafting my profile. I selected pictures that showed just enough body that a man wouldn't be surprised I am plus-sized or have graying hair or any other sign of "imperfection." The first week my matches seemed at least possible. Tall and bearded Black men with similar education levels to mine not too far from the city. I got zero messages, but finally when the messages did start about two weeks in they were from older white men who seemed more interested in my "chocolate" skin and me being the first Black woman they'd dated. Or at least publicly. They said these things like they were prizes and I should be honored to be on the receiving end of these "compliments." I wasn't, and shortly after, I canceled the subscription and went back to radio silence.

I promised my therapist to keep the apps on my phone for at least a few weeks, but by our next session they are deleted. My therapist laughs deeply because over the growing weeks of our Saturday video chats, she understands me. She also says, and I've said the same thing, that I have no real concept of dating. I've been in a series of long-term relationships that have gone from zero to one hundred. It has been rare that I've casually dated. Most of the time, I am mentally in a relationship before the very first date and sometimes the men go along for the ride. On the apps, before I can even consider opening a message or matching with someone, I am already thinking of how much time I must invest or what happens when things go wrong or how a relationship may unfold.

During a recent rewatch of *He's Just Not That into You*, I stop the film just about halfway in because suddenly the main character, Gigi, begins to make me angry. She spends the opening segment of the film pining over whether or not a man she's gone on one date with will call. She analyzes and frets over his words and actions until she works herself into a frenzy. I know this is all played for laughs, but it stings to see her repeatedly checking her phone, rushing through the interactions and friendships that are actually important, and losing bits and pieces of herself in a rushed pursuit to be coupled. Even if this is a situation I hope to avoid, there is still a swirling cloud of romance that exists in all of the toxic storylines in the movie. There is still so much possibility for a happy ending that I've overlooked each of the heartbreaks in every viewing of the film before this.

I met my high school sweetheart and declared him the love of my life. I met the boyfriend of my twenties and settled into a very serious live-in relationship within two years. I got married to a different man a little over three years after the previous relationship ended. We divorced not too long after. Then came the situationships lasting a few months to damn near ten years. There has never, in the history of my adult life, been a season of getting to know someone and deciding a relationship with them isn't for me. It is always *I like you, you are mine, we are done*. And if I am being honest, it has also been *I like you, you play me, I cry*. Or *you like me, I get skittish, I run*. It all ends up crossing the same finish line: alone.

I need to learn to settle, not into some half-assed coupling, but into the idea that everything in my life doesn't have to be all-or-nothing. This is more difficult for me than I can explain. Somehow I manage to love the idea of love without actually knowing if I've ever truly felt it. What it feels like is chasing after those first moments over and over again and hoping they will manifest into something more substantial. This is a sickness, really.

Still, in every relationship I've felt just that way—lonely—even in the coupling. My therapist and I chat about how perhaps my fear of the dating apps is because it is difficult to open up and trust someone new. I suppose this is a part of it. In hindsight, I know I've held my tongue too much; lowered my expectations; let pain be heaped upon me in order to be anything but unchosen. But I have also been just as bad—in my silent slinking away; in my emotional affairs to fill the gaps of what I felt was missing.

· · · · ·

I TELL MY THERAPIST THAT what I miss most about being truly coupled is the mundane intimacy of it all. To have someone in the periphery of my life. There are moments when my mind disappears into the daydreams of the love life I wish I had. I relay to her that these cravings come at odd times. The loneliness and longing hit me when I least expect it. These daydreams play out like movie montages. Sometimes they are scenes from a life I used to have—when I can remember how what was once solid turned to dust in my grasp. But mainly they come at unremarkable times. When I am taking the clothes from the dryer—their warmth softening my fingertips until they feel numb and buzzing like static. They come because I remember that the clothes are only mine. There is no man's hoodie to slip over my head or his lingering cologne on the collar of a shirt or some ratty T-shirt I want him to get rid of like in the buildup toward the midpoint breakup in a love story.

My life has never happened in any way I should have ever believed this was possible. But I know so keenly that at some point I was almost there. I felt the warmth of it—of what I wanted—and it was so very ordinary. Probably a life most would want to escape. A life of routines built upon love. Like favorite takeout places every Friday night. Grocery runs and sitting in the car just a little while before heading in for the night. Of open windows and moving closer in the chill. Of comfortable silence and minor angers and long-lasting connection. I've never wanted an extraordinary love. I just wanted it to be real.

Most recently this longing manifested as I was standing at the sink washing peaches for a cocktail and charcuteric day. I decided, after months of solitude in my home, to have friends over as a way to invite the outside in. I spent weeks buying all the trimmings for this gathering; scrubbing down my apartment; arranging flowers in a bright spray on the coffee table. In a rom-com I would be hosting this gathering with my significant other. I'd set the table and eventually find myself next to him with my fingers dancing across the back of his head. But like I said, my life has never truly been that way.

While I was washing the peaches, I became absent from myself and for a time I was anywhere besides at the sink staring out between the blinds. In those moments I was nowhere else, just daydreaming about a lover in another room. In that absence, I imagined what my renewed domestic life would be. For the sake of my heart, I imagined it was peaceful and consistent. I imagined it circled upon the shared understanding that consistent is not boring. Consistent is what you make it. When the peaches were rinsed, I was back in my body. Back in my quiet life. A single woman wrestling with solitude.

There's a scene in *He's Just Not That into You* that shows a little girl being told that a boy is sometimes mean to you if he likes you. I think we are supposed to follow the logic that there is always bitter before the sweet and if you can just swallow the first mouthfuls of it, then all will be well. This is bullshit. It is bullshit because swallowing and swallowing and swallowing the bitter makes you immune to the harm, and before you know it you are happy to think this is how you are to be fed. With every rom-com, romance novel, and love song I've ingested, I've learned to ignore the poison for the sake of the "cure."

This is what this manufactured romance has made me forget. What happens when it all fades? At the end of the dinner party in my daydream where do I and this imaginary lover stand? Does he help with the dishes and clear the table? Does he settle beside me and massage the spot just at the base of my neck where all the tension builds? Or am I even more alone than when I started?

• • • • •

REMEMBER IN *Waiting to Exhale* when Robin and Savannah are bonding poolside? They are chatting about whether or not Savannah should show a little more faith in Kenneth, her ambiguous and very married love interest in the film. Savannah looks in control, as she does in most of the run-time. Her white T-shirt shimmers in the sun as she peers over her shades at Robin. And Robin is what she has been the entire movie—wholly beautiful, feminine, poised, and a little sad at the edges. Her shoulders are baking in the sun above a strapless top—a stark contrast from Savannah's T-shirt—and that is another part of Robin. Openness. One that unfurls as the movie continues on.

All around the two of them is the bustle of others and the kinetic energy of a summer day. As Robin spools out the story of how she came to be in Phoenix, Arizona, she tells it like she is reading from a page. There is a haze over the fine details of the story, but all of it is there in the way she looks far into the distance and the way her face slackens into softness. Then her brows knit and her lips flatten and reinflate into something beyond a pout. Robin's face shadows for a moment and then it, and her voice, flatlines.

Robin spins the brokenness of her heart like it was some sort of dark fairy tale. While it is clear all of what she is saying belongs to her and no one else, Savannah lets Robin tell it as Robin sees fit to make sure it is heard. She knows Robin is often silenced and pushed aside when she tries to express how she feels. And perhaps in that fairy tale is a pain Savannah recognizes. In the quiet around them, the two disappear into the crevices of Robin's story. No matter how dissimilar these women appear to be on the surface, they are kindred.

Savannah's mother wanted her to settle into a suffocating space waiting for Kenneth to live his life in order for Savannah to give him hers. The phrase "He's a good man" is repeated over and over again, and all she has to do is wait for him to be ready. *All* she has to do is stand by while he neatly wraps up the frayed edges of his life. *All* Savannah has to do is have a little more faith that she will finally be chosen.

As the movie continues, Robin keeps believing that some-day her prince will come. She tries and tries to find someone who really loves her but keeps getting sucked back into the toxic love she has with Russell. Then Troy throws those damn oranges at her in his hot-ass leather vest. But I guess this kind of brings me full circle. He drunkenly shouts up at her on the balcony about Black women. How they complain that no one wants them and that's why he, and others like him, date white women.

Sometimes on the apps I run into profiles of men who starkly remind potential partners that Black women are not their preference. That we should not hold our breath for a response. Should expect nothing but to be ignored or insulted if we cross the line and swipe right or like or message them. And God forbid you are not fine.

* * * * *

ONE SATURDAY MORNING I WAKE UP way too early, and there is nothing to do except putter around the apartment until it is time to do chores and start my pending session. In the kitchen, the stove knobs are soaking in equal parts water, soap, and bleach. Where the smell of cleaning does not fill the air, there is music and birds chirping in the open windows. In a recurring daydream I've found myself standing at my sink on a morning like this when the weight of another body sidles up behind me and wraps me tightly. I can almost feel the tenderness of this, and it makes me so overwhelmingly sad. I fall back into my default motto, "I am okay. I don't need anyone." I tend to say this to myself over and over again even if I know it not to be true.

I mentioned to my therapist in a prior session that I have a type, and she tasked me with making a list of what I want. The first week the list concentrated almost exclusively on the physical traits I find attractive in a man, with only a casual mention of his hobbies. It was like Robin's declaration in the opening of *Waiting to Exhale*—I like pretty boys with big sticks. She said a whole lot of nothing about something. Maybe I should have modeled my list after Savannah's. Integrity. Compassion. A sense of purpose.

My therapist challenged me to go deeper. What do I want to experience in a relationship? What do I need to feel safe with a man? What are the dealbreakers? What don't I want because I've had it before and it hasn't worked out? What's been missing? I've been happy with the bare minimum for so long I was afraid I didn't know anything other than *just be nice to me*. It took me a few days to come up with twelve items. What I came up with was a list that was basic for some but workable for me.

But what I truly think I fear, and why that first list was so scarce, was that I was not quite convinced I had the right to expect more. That in this aging body, this childless body, this imperfect body, sometimes scraps are better than starving. I think I have convinced myself I do not want, or can live without, the soft romance I grew up reading in novels or watching in movies because I've somehow been tricked into believing, and have allowed myself to also believe, I am not worthy.

How I've fought against the desire to have a hand on an exposed slip of my skin—feeling the weight of fingers digging into my flesh. Or knowing my entire being is imprinted into a man's memory so he can love me fully. I have convinced myself that none of this desire can be real because it has never seemed an actual possibility. But I've felt the edges of it. A quiet proposal in front of a Christmas tree in the glow of golden lights. Waking to a birthday cake full of candles shining in the face of a man who may have possibly tipped over into loving me. A few late evenings with an arm slung across my waist and me being pulled closer when I dared to move. But the context of each of these were like islands in a vast ocean. Simply a place to rest before being battered again in the waves.

What do I say about a sense of longing that seeps all the way into my bones some days? It seems no matter how uncomfortable the apps make me, they at least create a bridge to a land of possibility. Maybe in the brack of profiles and pictures there will be someone who appears like a message in a bottle saying, "Here I am. I've been waiting." I keep bobbing around in the waves—up and down through each false start, hoping against hope I will find a shore. I used to think this would save me. Thought perhaps this would make the way-too-empty spaces of my heart flood. It is only in the briefest of moments that I can process this as a recipe for disaster. Instead of waiting for someone to rescue me, I should remember I do not need to be saved. I just need a solid place to rest.

· · · · ·

FROM TIME TO TIME when I'm at work, the elders I speak with like to bless me. Sometimes they peer around my computer and try to catch a glimpse of my fingers dancing across the keys. I know they are searching for a ring. They like to tell me how kind I am and how good of a mother and a wife I must be. There is always shock when I say I am none of these things. When I reveal this, most of them slump back into their chairs a bit and glance momentarily at the jumble of papers in front of them. They shuffle their Social Security cards, birth certificates, and notices. But some of them glance up from their documents to tell me how much of a shame it is that I have no children or man to call my own. I just need to wait a little while longer, they say. Patience is a virtue.

But I must be honest when I say I am so very worried that before I slip from this world I will not feel this type of love. Perhaps I would feel differently if I had not seen the possibility of it all firsthand—and in real tones, not the overly saturated vision we are led to believe love should be. I have a habit of thinking and writing about my parents tenderly because they have been the blueprint for what a relationship can be. As are so many couples in my orbit. My sister and cousins and aunts and uncles and friends all circle love that is more grounded than the love in any movie or song. I nearly grasped these same feelings, but maybe not really. It was for the best that coupling, really all of the relationships I've ever known, ended if only to open me up for what may be something greater.

• • • • •

AN HOUR AGO, and still five more until my session, I slid from bed and slipped on a housedress, wrapped a scarf about my head, and brushed my teeth while my back unknotted itself from sleep. Now I stare into the mirror as the foam builds in my mouth. When I rise from spitting it into the sink, my face is framed. My father says I look more like my mother with each passing year. I think my body does too.

I search for the teardrop mole dead center of my breasts but find only the littering of them across my shoulders and neck, with a tiny one finding a home just below my right ear. I see my forehead starting to crease like hers, the silver entwining itself between the darkness of my hair, and the carve of her smile between the lines on my cheeks. I remark now, having lived nearly forty-four years on this earth, that one breast is slightly bigger than the other, that they are softer and more malleable than I remember. I marvel at my body some mornings like this—all that it's survived and all the ways it's grown.

I think of my mother at this age and how our lives seem so far apart. How visible she must have been to the world. A woman married, a mother of two, a child among ten, so many other ways she was gifted to the world. I think of how at this age I would have already raised a daughter of twenty-three who was freshly out of college and another daughter about age eleven. If I was her I would have owned a place in the world and been anchored solidly into the earth. But I am not. I feel like I am twisting in the wind—completely and utterly free in ways I never asked for or expected. I tell myself this is fine most days when I look into the mirror. But I've learned that sometimes you've got to lie to yourself to survive.

While I slather on moisturizer, I wonder if with each passing year it will become more and more difficult for me to find a partner. And whether or not I will be of the mind and heart to take a hand that may one day be extended to me in love and kindness. When I look at my face and body in the mirror I know that with each additional dimple, roll, wrinkle, or pound I am to believe that there is less hope. I worry I've been painted into a corner for so long that I wouldn't know healthy love if it was directly in front of me and that I will be willing to accept anything that comes along.

• • • • •

WRIST DEEP INTO A SLOSH of bleach, water, and soap, I scrub the remnants of spaghetti sauce from the knobs. Google plays a mix in the background and soon I am singing loudly because, as I am alone in the apartment, no one can hear me. I sacrifice some of the notes for silence and belt out the others my alto holds steady. My fingers have grown slick and I sniffle in the strong scent of clean before rinsing the knobs and replacing all four of them before their respective burners. The shuffle and slap of my flip-flops carry me between the kitchen and the bathroom, where I dash another splash of bleach into the bathtub then squeeze in the toilet bowl cleaner. The sun blazes outside, so the housedress makes a quick pass over my brow to wick away the sweat.

Above the bathroom mirror a collection of scents lords over the tile. In my advancing age I've gotten a bit obsessed with curating a rotation of signature scents—I tell myself that I want to be some combination of a classically dressed woman and an octogenarian art teacher. How I smell is just one layer of achieving this. Conventional beauty advice tells me to put my best foot forward by learning what looks best on my body, how to hide wrinkles, and how to age gracefully while not really aging at all. But this is all I've got. I pull down a bottle and spray a bit of its scent on my skin to chase away the bleach smell before I finally notice the sink below has yet to drain.

I keep musing as I run a bit more water into it to see if just maybe the slow drain will somehow correct itself. It doesn't, and maybe this is just like the patterns I am trying to shake. I know what doesn't work. Know what kind of relationships I've let into my life. Know keenly I am far too old to keep up this cycle if I want some shot at external, romantic happiness. But there I am still in the same place hoping some minor changes have shifted an entire adulthood of the same decisions. To be honest, I've settled so deeply into what I'm used to that it is difficult to see beyond what I've always known.

The urge to cry washes over me, but I refuse. I cry entirely too much about things I am not sure I am actively trying to change. Or can be changed. I've cried on my sofa. In the bathtub. In the bed. In my car. Any and everywhere. *I'm a robot*, I sniffled out one Friday night while watching DJ Jazzy Jeff spin on Twitch. *A goddamn crying robot*. I don't even know why I was crying. What in the cutting and scratching was so emotionally triggering that I couldn't help but be overwhelmed? A wave of depression had just crashed over me, I guess. Maybe another weekend of aloneness with no end in sight was the tipping point.

The toothpaste foam trapped in the sink is floating on the surface, and I sprinkle heavy shakes of Comet until everything is blue-green and I am choking. I can feel the grit of the chemicals now—note how good it feels against my fingertips and how it makes my throat and nose itch and contract. I start to scrub until my shoulders ache and all the frustration slides down my arms and pools with the stagnant water. The water is now wrist-deep, and the slow drain gives me time to walk away. Enough time to wander from the bathroom and gather myself along with an armful of solutions. Baking soda and vinegar. Drano. A plunger and a rattail comb. One of these will work.

I need to clean up this mess before my session because I want my mind to be clear. I want to be able to articulate why it feels like I have been drowning this week and how the very valid feelings I have are so routine that I am tired of feeling them. That I know what to say to myself to combat them but I can't seem to put the words into action.

I toy with the idea of downloading the apps again just to give them a real try. It's the smallest step I can make. But what will I say? *Hi! I'm Athena. A divorced, childless woman who probably won't trust you and if you show too much interest I'll probably run. I need space, but not too much. I may get way too attached to you, but I won't put too much pressure on you because I'm afraid you'll leave. And can you please be bearded, tall, and nearly completely emotionally unavailable because I like a challenge and because I want to figure out how you tick. If that's okay you can text me, but please don't call.*

I sprinkle the baking soda into the sink liberally—watch it tint with the Comet traces and the foam. Hear the vinegar fizz and fizz and bubble, but the water remains the same. Next the plunger. I prime it and use all the strength left in my arms to pump and pull until there is a splash of hair and murky gray water and deflated soap bubbles. I wonder where it all comes from and fear sticking my hand into it to scoop out the debris. There's a story in there somewhere. Something about clearing out the heart or the mind, but it's all just bullshit. All of my hard work will look like the bullshit pouring from the drain, but the water will go down. Slower. Then faster. Then gone.

One Great Thing

I n Alliance, Ohio, at the apex of River Street, Webb Avenue, and Jennings Road, Crybaby Bridge stretches across a small section of the Mahoning River. It sits among a triangle of streets extending toward the outer limits of town and offers a trio of paths to explore. But this is no ordinary bridge. Rumor has it the bridge is a dumping ground for unwanted babies. Depending on which tale you choose to believe, children are tossed into the water by desperate mothers or the Klan. Legend says you can hear the babies' cries among the trickle of the water and the sounds of trains in the distance. Cars parked on the bridge stall and die. The story says maybe the curious will find a hand or footprint stamped onto their vehicles when they depart. The legend teases believers that sometime after midnight those brave enough to stand on the bridge or the banks of the river below can hear women and their children. I've never tried to hear their cries, but I do know regret and the feeling of empty hands.

"I've been thinking about having a baby," I venture.

The potential father is my best friend. He is a brilliant musician and producer. Intelligent and witty. A bit of an asshole but curious about the world and cultured to boot. On paper he is the perfect candidate. He's offered me a chance at motherhood because I want it and he thinks I would be good at it. I think his offer started as a joke with me on a rant about feeling regret about not having a baby and how now the time to do so had long since passed. I was beyond my self-imposed deadline of thirty-three despite his instance that my time had not passed. Modern medicine has come a long way, he thinks. And being over forty isn't necessarily the end of fertility.

I pull into a parking space in front of my building as the last bit of light is leaving the sky. I am far away from Crybaby Bridge, but children still haunt me. I started making a list of names in my head. Baldwin, Ethan, Langston, and Ellison for boys. Zora, Simone, Olivia, and Andromeda for girls. The thought of having babies consumes me sometimes, and I worry as if I already have one—about schools, a larger vehicle, purchasing a home, moving back to Ohio. There is also the fear I am not complete or that maybe I am missing out on some rite of passage. That I'm not really a whole woman. I worry my insides have dried up and it is far too late to even try. There were years I thought having children was the next natural step. Education. Wedding. Husband. Baby. A life complete.

"He offered me a baby," I say plainly. Like this is normal. Like it makes sense to willingly walk into a mess just to figure out if this is what I really want. But he's serious. I know he is. All I have to do is say yes.

My mother remarks it is my decision, but she doesn't think it's the best idea. Last week an old acquaintance told me maybe I should get a dog. I've been told by others I have a good life and children will only disrupt it. I've been told I am selfish or impatient or set in my ways. I've been told children would ruin my life. I say to my mother that I've always felt I am good at many things but I've never been exceptional at any of them. I try to explain that maybe being a mother was my chance at one great thing, and now it's far too late. I don't know what to do with these feelings. I want to push them away or hold them close until I figure out what I actually want. I will be the first to admit I don't really have a handle on any of this longing. I just know there is regret mixed with fear under the shadow of a ticking clock.

One of the legends of the bridge says a mother tossed her child over the railing only to be hit with instant regret. Born out of wedlock, the child would have never been accepted by her family or the community at large. The path to motherhood is sometimes conditional. Filled with regret, the mother leapt into the air, a scream left behind, trying to retrieve what she'd thrown away. Between the solid ground of the bridge and the murky water below, she perished. The legend doesn't mention if she and the baby were reunited in their ghostly forms.

· · · · ·

YEARS AGO, I read about the leftover women of China. This segment of women, unmarried and childless beyond their twenties, have no real place in society. They are often overlooked and chastised for their decisions. No matter their accomplishments, being a mother and a wife trumps them all. I think I fall into this category now. Divorced and solidly middle-aged without much change in sight.

In an updated article about these types of women in the *Atlantic* in 2020, one of them, Qiu Hua Mei, comes to symbolize the pitfalls in this way of thinking. "Throughout history, and across cultures, women's bodies have been treated as a communal resource for creating the citizens of the future—and therefore states try to control women's lives to influence their reproductive capacity,"[10] writes Helen Lewis. "Today, it manifests more subtly as social pressure suggesting that 'fulfillment' comes only from marriage and children." Yet there are still boundaries to these goals. Are you married? To whom? By what age? What is your income? Your education? Too many questions in and about a womb that belongs to only one person.

Twilight has washed over the block as I exit the car and start the short trek to my building's stairs. There is something inside of me that wishes to find tiny handprints on the interior of the window or the streak of small fingers in the dust coating the door. Like something had been trying to hang on or get out. I kind of wish for a babble in the wind. This hush of time between work and home seems magical some days and like the cusp of sadness on others. The commuters have disappeared and the street is emptied now. The city breaks with a siren a few streets over—the wail of it echoes like cries over water.

• • • • •

THE MAHONING RIVER FLOWS eventually to the Ohio and Mississippi Rivers before emptying its secrets into the Gulf of Mexico. Legend be truth, a wash of babies floats along with it—carrying the shame and desperation of countless mothers. What drives a community to spin a tale of such tragedy? To look down into the brown depths of the water and see small faces ghosting below the lap? The legend is about escape even if I don't understand the actions. Perhaps if we can put air to

---

10 https://www.theatlantic.com/international/archive/2020/03/leftover-women-china-israel-children-marriage/607768/.

these stories, maybe something comes to light about ourselves. I'm not sure what the light will expose, though. I just know that through the act of telling, of recording, of archiving these types of tales, we make an exchange with the world, bartering our joy and pain for a bit more solid ground.

I develop an interest in the bridge and bring my father into the research fold. I've run into a dead end on YouTube and Google. Small towns have a way of holding their secrets, but if you ask for them from the inside, there are many stories to be told. What I want to know now is the truth from the ones who lived it. My father and I both share a question on Facebook. *What do you know about Crybaby Bridge?* There are links and comments and no real consensus. Some say the bridge is not the one I know—that it exists in another part of town. Others say they've only experienced haunting presences in the Jewish cemetery not too far away from the bridge. Still others say they've never heard of it but it all sounds terrible. The legend is like the ghosts it honors—some people see it and others don't. Some people believe in the possibility of something they can't quite see because they have a wholehearted belief that just because something isn't within your grasp, it can't be true.

The legend of Crybaby Bridge spans at least thirty cities in my home state and even more across the nation. The stories morph to fit those towns, but the premise remains the same—loss of something precious and the haunting it leaves behind. The truth, at times, needs a buffer to come to the surface. It's why we tell fables, why we find ways to wrap the truth in fantasy. People need something to hide behind if we are really going to tell the truth plainly. The stories are a stopgap between daydreams where reality lives and a moment when all that is perfect morphs into something too much to handle. If I believe the legend, I can clearly see the ghosts of young mothers teetering over the edge of the railings. I can make out the squirming bundles in their arms—bucking softly and cooing. I can maybe understand the chill when they discover their desire to love isn't quite enough to make a difference in what life has laid in their paths.

I think the same type of doubt is what my mother and friend believe about me having a child. Maybe they think I can't see beyond my own desire and before I know it, I will be standing on the edge of the world waiting to drop my troubles into the abyss. My personal Crybaby Bridge. I imagine they knew I'd pictured something so grand and good on the horizon that I couldn't see what was just below the surface. I thought simply that because I wanted a child so badly it had to become reality. Maybe the one great thing escaped me because it wasn't meant to be. It doesn't make me any less of a woman or more of a failure. It's simply a dream that didn't come true.

· · · · ·

WHEN THE PARANORMAL HUNTERS compile their notes about Crybaby Bridge, they often place it next to a cemetery. I suppose this heightens the tension, the quiet, and the atmosphere. This is not the truth. The cemetery is a mile away and sweeping with grave markers and monuments—where these lost children would have had proper burials. A little piece down the road there would be mourning in daylight instead of secret death waiting to be washed away into nothing. At the corner of those three streets, on a blue-gray bridge now rusting, nothing is proper. Nothing is buried. Instead, everything floats away from the source—picking up currents and speed until it can no longer be saved.

• • • • •

A FEW MONTHS AFTER Crybaby Bridge washes from my memory, my friend Lara texts me. She's been reading about my deprivation tank experience and thinks she has something for me to consider. "Eigengrau is a German term that roughly translates to 'intrinsic gray' or 'own gray.' When deprived of light—as in when our eyes are closed, or when we are in darkness with our eyes open—we are unable to perceive true blackness, and rather, perceive eigengrau," she texts into our chat. When she shares this, the world outside is the dull gray of January on the East Coast. Low clouds roll over the buildings in my neighborhood and even though this unusual winter has no snow, the air is heavy. It's thick, like something wants to break through but can't. Like the sky knows there should be wet flakes and drifts piling the streets four floors below my window.

Back home in Ohio, many winters ago, I had a red sled. Fitted with brakes and a singular headlight, it made swooping down the hills at a park not too far from my house more fun than it should have been. I careened down those slopes—toward a small footbridge and a brick square of a bathroom—pulling at the black handle to slow the whole thing down. For the rush down the hill, the trudge back to the top could be forgotten as could the burn in my chest as I tried to breathe icy air. This is what the sky feels like decades into the future. Oppressive with light just on the other side of the gray. Sometimes a white cloud breaks the swath of nothingness—perhaps a bird somewhere in the distance circling one of the bare trees.

From my sofa I can see between different trees and the brick buildings along the block. It's a little after two, and the doldrums are settling in. This is when I would give anything to feel the rush of my body letting go and hovering over the plastic seat of my sled for just a moment before gravity pulls me back down and the wind pushes me forward. A scream on the cusp of my lips and the cold drawing tears from my eyes. But this is not childhood.

When I can't remember the name of the park, I call my father and he tells me that nothing is the same. The Memorial Park I've known is gone. The basketball courts have been removed as have the single pavilion and swings and monkey bars. Gone, too, is the square bathroom building where one summer a swarm of carpenter bees kept me trapped even if they likely would not sting. Now there is a skate park under the shadow of a block of senior apartments, a McDonald's, and a gas station. Still, we both remember the park was the best place to sled. The hills at Silver Park didn't quite stack up—their pitches too low to give much of a thrill. I search for something in his voice when I mention the sled and I know he remembers it too. I want to feel deeply what it must spark to know his daughter holds on to the memory of it so long after she lived it. A bit of plastic and some cords that have long since been scrapped are anchored in her mind.

The two of us remember more of this hill than we do of Crybaby Bridge, and I wonder if this is where I should focus. That maybe what is important isn't the absence of my own parental memory, but something beyond that. This regret, a hum sometimes deep in my womb, is something I can never fill. And dissecting some perceived wrong turn or missed opportunity can do nothing other than make me feel guilty and mournful of a life that never was.

The Daily Journal

"To those concerned: This book is just a few recorded events or happenings in my lifetime."

—the journal of WILLIE MAE HORNE
passed to her daughter Sharon Dixon upon
Mrs. Horne's passing in April 2022

DEAR ME,

I want to feel like I belong somewhere. (11/04/2011)

I will say that I am being cautious because I don't want to mistake my loneliness of the last nine months for attraction. (08/03/2012)

I want to be a wild woman. A red lipstick–wearing, sexy, bold, wild woman. I'm trying to figure out how to be that. (11/21/2012)

Loneliness will make you do strange things. (09/12/2013)

The loneliness is powerful today . . . I feel like I am starving. (09/22/2013)

What is done is done. What is will remain. (10/30/2013)

I don't want to be singular anymore. (11/11/2013)

I've yelled at God three nights now. He hasn't listened to me in three years and quite frankly, I'm starting to question his existence. (11/13/2013)

Now it's just me being piecemeal for another's pleasure. (03/10/2014)

Sometimes I still feel in stasis. (07/30/2014)

I think I'm meant to be fucking alone. (08/07/2014)

I'm tired of being parceled out. (08/19/2014)

So, I'm sitting here at a bar in Atlanta having a drink. In this moment I am feeling both empowered and alone. I'm feeling empowered because I've spent the last two days enjoying myself. (09/27/2014)

As I begin to think I will be single for a very long time, things like this will be an occurrence more and more. And in the end, what's wrong with this life? (09/27/2014)

There is comfort in airports—a shared experience. I should fly more often. (09/28/2014)

Vivid, visceral, and engaging. I wrote in another journal back in January that Aunt Mary said I had a life she wished she did. (09/28/2014)

I'm back to thinking my desperation is so palpable that the vultures circle me and I'm starved for touch so their pecks and bites seem like a caress. (10/01/2014)

I think I figured out what's wrong with me. I'm invisible. People don't see me. Or I should say they only see me when they need me. That is probably the most painful realization I've come to in the past few years. Who checks in on me? Who thinks of me and wants to make sure I am okay? No one. I really am a solitary being. Like if I disappeared who'd notice? It's so easy for people to ignore me, to not respond to me, to forget me. (10/21/2014)

Today was a terrible day. The feeling of loneliness and sadness was so overwhelming today that I didn't know what to do. It's just that I feel like there is no end in sight. I always feel as if I'm not seen. (10/22/2014)

My dad made a point to me a long while ago. He said, "Just because someone looks happy doesn't mean they are." I have to believe that and remember that. What we usually see of others' lives are the highlights. All the bad, boring, and bullshit is hidden. (10/23/2014)

But then again, I could fall under the idea of the red thread that connects people who are meant to be. The thread may tangle and meander, but it never breaks. (10/31/2014)

And that's how you lose a man. Too many books. Too bougie. Too Black. Too much butt. Too much of too little. (04/09/2015)

I'm exercising demons over dinner and I'm oddly fine. (05/04/2015)

You know those stories about the solo humpback whale? She roams the ocean alone because the pitch of her call doesn't match the others and they can't hear her/connect with her. That's what I feel like. Like I'm shouting into the void and my voice is getting sucked into the abyss. (05/18/2015)

I feel like if I disappeared no one would blink an eye. (05/28/2015)

I've been hiding away from pretty much everyone and everything. The loneliness I thought I had in check is back in full force. It's so hard to see around, to see through. It seems insurmountable. (12/26/2015)

I think I'm becoming numb at some points and better at others. (12/26/2015)

I'm not really sure where I am headed next. I'm just really weary. Really tired. Like the idea of having a soft place in the world, a haven, is never going to happen. The world is a hard, scary place and those who have someone have no idea how lucky they are. (12/26/2015)

Love is still love. (02/19/2016)

Like we all serve a specific purpose. And that is how I've come upon the idea I am an emotional jump-off. (06/11/2016)

My life is always in a state of flux, but in this particular moment it feels good. Things are far from perfect, but I am so much better than I thought I would be five years ago. Despite hearing the complete opposite, I have value and I am worthy of a good life of my own design. I'm getting there slowly but surely. (06/16/2016)

And the sad part is we're the ones everyone assumes is always okay. I'm not. (06/29/2016)

I don't want to be lonely, but I guess that's what it is. (08/06/2016)

Do I like being alone? Of course not. Can I be? Sure! (09/22/2016)

One of my greatest fears is I will live my entire life alone and when I die there will be nothing for anyone to remember me by. Like if I was gone the world wouldn't blink. (10/17/2017)

Black don't crack, but it does wither. (02/09/2019)

It's said the meek shall inherit the Earth, but what about the humble? I remarked on Twitter one morning that in my quest to be humble, I'd become quite adept at kowtowing. (07/17/2019)

I don't know how to crack open my chest. What I do know how to do is open my mouth and let out a whimper that to me sounds like a roar. (12/09/2019)

Am I out of my depths? Where do I belong? (12/04/2020)

How can I find power in my past and present? What do I need to let go of in order to move forward? (12/18/2020)

I operate on a lower frequency that can be hard to hear at times. Like sonar waves. (08/13/2021)

I scream I'm here. Alive and whole and loved. I say look at my value. It was always there even if neither of us bothered to recognize it. (02/07/2022)

The World Is Ending and I Don't Want to Drink Alone

drink the moonshine clear as water on the bar cart until my vision is blurry. Until I pull the slosh of my body to bed where I will cry, deep and hard, until I find something to hold on to. Not hope. Not love. Just something that tells me to get up in the morning. I am afraid to die before I figure out what it is. Afraid to die before I find a heart in which to hide. The world continues to pile on. Death after death. Erosion after erosion. Evil after evil. Until the world is tired. Apathetic. Resigned.

I drink the vodka hidden in the back of the refrigerator behind reused juice bottles and milk that always goes bad. I drink it with Sharkberry Fin Kool-Aid and Chinese delivery lemonade because it's smoother that way. The vodka was a birthday gift from when I still commuted to a desk that once a year was decorated in celebration of me. It reminds me of hugs and breakrooms and potlucks so I grip the glass tighter just to feel something against my skin. I feel like I am starving, trying to fill my belly and my mind with memory.

I drink the wine my friend passed through the window of her car, a mask hiding her smile while mine hid the same. How we talked about the death of a superhero and how the year held nothing sacred. When I drink the wine during yet another video call, the world catches up with me and my body agrees it is running on fumes and lack of sleep. I find myself fainting into shattered glass and wondering when I lost control.

I want to drink the small corner of mango rum left in the bottle from last Thanksgiving. It's been so long since the bottle has opened that the metal cap is nearly impossible to budge. I've tried it several times and I've resigned in my head that the bottle will be there when November comes. Break in case of emergency.

PART TWO
Out in the World

Double Exposure

My first- and second-grade school pictures,
Liberty Elementary School, Alliance, Ohio

few days before Jordan Peele's *Us* was released in the United States, I attended a special screening. I'd barely been able to watch the trailer because while I do not care much about gore in horror movies, anything that plays with the mind terrifies me. This is because I am a chronic overthinker and can't stop myself from re-creating the fear in my head on a loop. Like when I watched *Sinister* for the first time. I'd been the least bit impacted by the murder and more afraid of reflections in computer screens or what could be possibly be lurking in the everyday items I touched.

The prospect of there being something just slightly unseen in my world terrified me so much more than bodies being shredded by lawn mowers, drowned, or hung. I'd made it through *The Exorcist* just fine, but *Rosemary's Baby* stuck with me. The very real possibility of the stability of my mind being questioned and being dragged to the edge of sanity without ever being touched was hard to shake.

My friend Marisol, who has a passion for all things horror, tagged along to see the movie with me. She'd bought me a pair of scissor earrings to mimic the signature weapon of the Tethered in the film and she was just as excited as I was frightened, I think. I figured if I got too scared, she was there to ground me. And at the very least I had someone to lean into when I couldn't bear to look at the screen. By the time we made it out of the ticket line and into the packed theater, the only decent seats we could find were about three rows from the front.

I settled in, shaking and tightly wound as if somehow I was going to be sucked into the screen. And I was fine . . . until Adelaide's childhood secret continued to be revealed. As the story and the characters continued to move more deeply underground and the lines between what seemed to be real and what was actually true continued to blur, I knew I was going to be thinking about the movie for a very long time. It wasn't because it had suddenly catapulted to my list of favorites but because a part of me felt seen in Red. Then seen in Adelaide, but unsure about which one I really was.

There's a switch. In the depths of the hall of mirrors the very real Adelaide is attacked by, and replaced by, her doppelganger. The little girl on the other side of the mirror grins like she knows all the secrets of the world, then snakes her tiny hands around another tiny throat, and slips both of them back to the other side. Only one of them comes back. Red's transition into Adelaide's life isn't seamless—she doesn't speak—but eventually she catches up with who she is supposed to be, and no one is the wiser. Red comes fully to the surface, both figuratively and literally, and takes the life meant for the other little girl now trapped below.

· · · · ·

EACH YEAR BETWEEN ELEMENTARY and high school, Lifetouch came to our school district for picture day. For my mother this was a show. For me it was a day to be a doll. I'd always been well dressed and cared for. Hair and jewelry and matching shoes, but I really didn't care. I was happy in baggy turtlenecks and wide-legged jeans shredded from dragging on the ground. Picture day was for dressing, though. In one second-grade photo I am smiling without my two front teeth in a zoo animal shirt. Another year my mother instructed me to duck into the bathroom right before my turn in line and slip a blue and white sailor hat onto my head. And there I am in the photo—hat jauntily to the side. Each of these snapshots, including my senior pictures in which I posed with a face full of Mary Kay makeup and pineapple waves, were equal parts me and equal parts me wearing what I'd been told looked good. I didn't care much for fashion. Could not care less about my hair, and I most certainly did not like makeup.

There is only one photo in all those years I love. My tenth-grade photo when I looked not too happy and not too sad, and I remember being enamored with how pretty I felt that day. And that was unusual. Because I always felt awkward in my body. And my mind. Like the person looking back at me in a mirror couldn't possibly be the real reflection of the person doing the looking. Even now, old enough to be the mother of the girl in that photo, I feel like my age and how seasoned I am are decades apart.

These pictures, I guess, show how I've always felt. Split between what is supposed to be and what really is. One angle a smile and the other something a little more dampened. Not sad necessarily. Not evil or bad. Just melancholy and most certainly detached. Able to go through the motions more than anything. Even then, way back in the elementary school photos above, I lived in some sort of duality. Halfway on the path of what a good girl should be and always wanting to veer off into the opposite direction. Or to be left alone. But to also be the center of attention. I've always been a kind of odd balance of a child, somewhere between wanting to be a ghost or a deity.

In the book of school memories tucked away in my desk drawer, the handwriting of my teachers say things like "a pleasure to have in class" and "chatty in the hall with Greta." They say I'm almost gifted but not enough to be in the special class. That I'm in the ninety-ninth percentile in vocabulary on the Iowa test but below average in math. My handwriting is not the best and I hold the pencil way too close to the lead. But I am a good girl—easy to teach and most certainly not a lick of trouble to be had.

What I see, and what I don't, neatly cataloged away is my real feelings. I see the photos, ribbons, and awards, and I see the handwriting of my mother documenting each school year as it ended for the summer. The handwriting gradually switches to mine over the course of the thirteen years the book contains. I feel so detached from this version of myself. Like this little girl was some sort of doll behind glass that I can never remember touching. I know this is me. I recognize my face in the photographs. I remember the teachers. I may even remember small details of the events that happened during those years. Like in my fifth-grade school play where I took the role of Mother Spaceman. There is the briefest flash in my memory of an upside-down fruit bowl covered in tin foil and balanced on my head. Or how I only remember my days in Latchkey because my mouth recalls the taste of the Super Donuts served before classes started. But there are times I try my best to remember things I think I should know, but I draw blanks. Some people have told me this is normal. That you can't remember everything, but it still seems so odd to me. What I do remember is hyperfocused, but the major plot points of my life seem shadowed.

•••••

LUPITA NYONG'O'S CHARACTER, Adelaide, stares off into the distance in one scene at the beginning of *Us*. Her family has just arrived at their summer home and they are settling in. Adelaide is apprehensive, it seems. But perhaps this is because her parents have both passed and this home, its traditions, and its memories are now hers to navigate with her own family even while she is still dealing with her childhood trauma. Her husband, Gabe, and their children, Zora and Jason, are bouncing energies off each other. There's the controlled rowdiness that comes with families just on the edge of being confined together for too long. Adelaide is eating strawberries while her family chatters around her while enjoying a fast-food meal. She's there, sure, but the light behind her eyes is gone. The fruit makes its way to her mouth slowly, and she takes a distracted bite that seems more habit than hunger. And in an instant she is back—fully connected to the life before her. This is not the first crack we see in the reveal of Red, but it is the one that makes the most sense to me. How you can be somewhere and nowhere at the same time.

When Adelaide's parents found her after the switch in the movie, they noticed only that she was no longer speaking. They began to work to help her, with the trauma of being lost as the root cause of it. But I always wonder how the most fundamental parts of her changing were swept away. How her tastes, patterns, and rhythms disappeared along with her voice. How could her parents not see the mimic?

It could be that no matter what you are to someone, you are never a blank slate. Who you are to them comes with a set of expectations like tintype into their minds and it is difficult to see what's really shifted if and when it does. You see yourself from the outside. Who they think you are versus who you've become. It's like what I imagine the real Adelaide felt on the wrong side of the mirror—knowing life was moving as it should just outside of her grasp until finally she had to find a way to connect to the life she now had or give up altogether.

While I was in elementary school and junior high, my report cards were full of good grades and praise. Tucked into the memory book along with years of these kinds of reports and comments are the proof of that. Certificates from Latchkey complimenting my good manners; another for not receiving any behavior check marks for the grading period; a handful of field day ribbons that show at some point I was athletic enough to win first place just as often as I got a prize for participating. There were a few missteps here and there, but for so long I seemed to be perfectly okay and perfectly average.

Still, I was perfectly split. There seemed to be the me everyone saw and rarely the me I felt was really true. This more truthful girl was a bit rebellious, held secrets and lies just as easily as she could smile and be a pleasure to know. I never did anything truly bad. I didn't steal or fight. I wasn't doing drugs or drinking underage. I wasn't having sex. Instead, I told little white lies at times about where I was going and who I was with. I snuck out of town to see my boyfriend. I sometimes let others be blamed for things I'd done because it was inconceivable to some adults I'd even misstep in those ways. I always kept myself clean so the trust between me and the adults in my life was never broken. In the grand scheme of life I don't think these lies had any real bearing on the world because it always continued as it should. But I felt a thrill to know this duality, no matter how vanilla it could seem from the outside, existed.

Ancient Egyptian mythology has a word, *ka*, that defines the idea of "a tangible 'spirit double' having the same memories and feelings as the person to whom the counterpart belongs."[11] The other side of us is not always an enemy. It can be a complement. What we see in the film *Us* about Adelaide's young son, Jason, is not innocence or childlike wonder. It is choice. And how the power of observation can change the dynamic of a relationship. Just as Red and Adelaide are sparring in the living room, Jason settles with his double, Pluto, in the closet. During the doppelgangers' assault on the Wilson family home, the tension builds so much that perhaps watchers can believe this is the end of the boy. That maybe Pluto will set fire to it all and Pluto and Jason will go up in flames together. But this doesn't happen. Jason works out a bridge between the two. He raises his hand and Pluto follows suit—not touching him, just mirroring his actions. This becomes important later on, but in

---

11 https://en.wikipedia.org/wiki/Doppelg%C3%A4nger.

this moment there is another switch. Not of physical bodies or life, rather of the future. Jason doesn't have to destroy Pluto. He can exist in parallel to him, sometimes switching directions and motions to put his other half exactly where he wants him.

Back when my first collection of essays debuted, I worried myself sick about what the people I loved would think of me. I wanted to hide from the knowledge that in these essays they would see me at my lowest. When I wanted to die. Would see my somewhat reckless cyber hookups. Would see I was barely holding myself together even when I seemed perfectly "myself." A few of them wondered if I thought they'd actually read the book because there was no way some of the stories in the pages could be me. One called me raunchy. But whatever was in that book was, and is, a part of me. This time, however, these were not little white lies. They were glaring truths about myself I was able to shift into the shadows until I could use them to my advantage. To heal myself. To inform those who needed to know. To connect with the like-minded. I no longer had to bury these things or pretend they did not exist. All I needed to do was figure out how to get this other half of myself to work in concert enough with this half to not destroy either of us.

•••••

IL BUON TEMPO VERRA is tattooed on the inside of my right wrist. Written in Latin, it translates to "The good time will come." I got it inked into my skin at a random tattoo shop one night in Youngstown, Ohio. I think it cost $80 and was paid for by a man who wasn't my boyfriend at the time. In the map of tattoos across my body, it is number eight.

I was living in Youngstown studying for my English degree, the second bachelors I'd earned at a state school in the roughly six

years since I graduated high school. I was writing and perform-
ing and building a life there. And I was also slightly obsessed
with eighteenth-century British poetry. Especially Shelley.

I say I got the tattoo on my wrist because it is a reminder
I am alive, still growing, and forever seeking better. But back
then I got it because I'd read somewhere Percy Bysshe Shelley had the phrase engraved on a ring he wore until the day
he died. The phrase became a rallying cry for where I stood.
Things weren't good and they weren't bad, but they could
always get better.

Somewhere in my studies, or obsession, I remember the
story of Shelley's death. How he'd been seeing his doppelganger for some time leading up to it, and just like in folklore
one of them had to die. The ghost story in my brain says that
Shelley drowned in an unseaworthy boat with impractical sails
during a storm. His decomposing body was not found until ten
days later when he washed ashore. A book of Keats's poems was
in his pocket.

The story goes he told people of a haunting version of
himself that would approach him and ask, "How long do you
expect to be content?" Just like most tend to believe seeing the
twin stranger of yourself means you must slay it or be replaced,
other versions circle the idea that seeing your doppelganger is a
harbinger of death. But death is relative.

Whether it be Shelley, or Adelaide, or Millicent Barnes in
The Twilight Zone episode "Mirror Image," each of these strangers are only the manifestations of those they haunt. Adelaide
was running from her own lies and ruin, so the only option was
to kill the ghost before it could kill her. Millicent was running
from the terror of seeing the other version of herself as much as
she was trying to escape the terror of no one else believing what

she'd seen. She was more a victim, or prey, of this stranger. Shelley's doppelganger had only asked him how long he could be content. It never asked for his life. Never seemed to wish him harm. The question of how much longer could he have been content only required an answer.

· · · · ·

THE BRUTAL CRUNCH OF RED'S NECK cracking under the pressure of Adelaide's chains at the end of *Us* is heartbreaking. Her gurgling whistle of "The Itsy Bitsy Spider" seems to be her making one final attempt to find a common thread with Adelaide. It is hard to hear. I probably give her more grace than most would allow her, though. More mourning of her end too. Red spent the entire runtime of the film hunting, maiming, and killing. But what of this was not caused by Adelaide? Her mirror opposite had built the perfect life. Husband. Babies. Summer homes. Friends. A body trained for dance. A voice. All of it a mockery of pretending to be exactly who she was not. And below the surface, plotting to make it back to what was once hers, was Red—the sacrifice for this mirage. She is the real Adelaide—the one choked and slipped to the other side of the mirror. The faux Adelaide had finally managed to erase her other half.

In the theater, still somewhat cowering beside Marisol, I cheered for the protagonist. I wanted her to save herself and her family. When she stared out into the darkness of their bedroom and told Gabe about the little girl who'd been chasing her closely her entire life, I had no reason to believe this was not true. When she danced around the underground classroom with Red, I winced at each clumsy movement of her body and felt her pain when everything she tried seemed to be countered without much effort. I knew how that felt. How the extension of her body seemed sizes too big or too small, but it was all she had.

When we left the theater, I was hoping silently for this "survivor" to be killed by her very own son. At the end, when Jason had stared blankly at her and his brows pushed together and he slid the Wolfman mask over his features, I hoped that when the screen faded to black it was because he got the revenge for the mother that should have been his. That somehow this child, a reflection of the upper and lower worlds, could do a better job of merging the two halves into a whole.

In Service of
the Algorithm

poiler Alert: *The Truman Show* ends like this.

Imagine Truman has been battered in a storm. Imagine him lashing himself to a boat with shaking hands, and fear nearly making him choke. He's been afraid of water nearly his entire life—respecting it because he knew the destruction it could bring no matter how beautiful it may be.

Imagine the storm rages on until he loses consciousness and the sky turns black behind his eyes—how bright it is when they open again. Now, imagine his boat drifts until it actually punctures the sky. The world comes to a sudden end, and this is finally his breaking point. Imagine him beating fists against what is supposed to be clouds and a brilliant blue sky. And then there is suddenly the voice of "God" and it knows Truman's name. "God" says Truman sweetly, and you can hear the smile in his voice. "God" tries to talk Truman into staying, but he balks. None of this is real. The voice of "God" is taunting, telling Truman it knows his every desire. This is not true. There's never been a camera inside Truman's head.

· · · · ·

I LIKE TO PRETEND I don't know I am being manipulated. I like to hide behind the idea that I choose where to engage, with whom to interact, and what to block from sight. There is only a tiny fraction of this knowledge that matters, but I cling to the handpicked pieces my mind tells me are important. Selective inspiration, if you will. This way I can build the world to my making and close my eyes against the knowledge I am being guided. Against the knowledge I'm being separated from what I really want even if I am no longer sure what that *really* is.

I watch a grainy clip of *The Truman Show*'s ending on You-Tube because I know that while I am writing about disconnect and isolation, the movie is a linchpin. And I think just maybe there is perhaps something to be said about choosing to stay in a bubble and not knowing you are in one. Nothing profound about how we as a society are hurtling toward oblivion and how soon we will be nothing more than vessels technology uses to maneuver the world. This seems a futile pursuit and honestly, I'm not doing much to change it. What matters a conversation about algorithms and how nothing we see is real if I'm not? I guess what I really want to dig into is why leaving the bubble is difficult or maybe how after so long of being marketed to and analyzed we don't know how to properly breathe outside it. How perhaps it is more comfortable to stay despite whatever sacrifice of self that decision may require.

I've been asking myself for months what it means to be disconnected and how even with the entirety of the world a few swipes away I feel this disconnect so keenly. I keep coming back to Truman because his world oddly makes sense to me even if, in my reality, I am technically fully aware. It's all illusion—all a ruse no matter the level of consciousness. Each day I log on and my view is curated for me. Somewhere software decides which of my friends and followers are most important and feeds me the latest about their lives. I see these curated feeds, and there is a rush or depletion of brain chemicals that make me happy or sad. I get jealous and competitive and passionate and even lonelier. I stop at times, glancing down at the phone in my hand, and know that what I'm feeling is envy of a life I think I want. To be popular and thin and rich and famous and important. I know these feelings are manufactured, but they are still heavy.

When I watch one too many clips, I know I am not clear of the algorithm that exists in everything I do. The programs have homed in on my viewing pattern, and soon all I see on the homepage of YouTube are more scenes from *The Truman Show* and clips from reality shows. The videos spark interest, and before I am conscious of my actions, I've opened several tabs to avoid missing any of the recommendations that pull me into a time suck. It is hard to understand how I still fall under the algorithm's sway when I know exactly what game is being played.

I know the lull and comfort of the algorithm—an easy life where there is no true required thought. The algorithm knows me. They've taken the digital scraps of me and pieced together a person who doesn't quite exist, but is exactly who I am. On Tumblr, which is a perfectly curated world I've created of my fandoms, the algorithm knows I am in my forties and I live in Pennsylvania. It shows me weekender bags and mid-century modern furniture ads that pique my interests. I screenshot them and tuck them away for later review. This unseen hand knows the life I want to create just as well as it knows the image I wish to project. It knows my insecurities and sends me missives about face waxing and weight loss and dating sites. Facebook does the same. There are days I watch so many 5-Minute Crafts videos, a hot glue gun is all I want to buy.

The algorithm moves me too. Without much thought, I accept recommendations for everything from news articles to people to follow. This is mostly effortless because I've become so immune to the subtle ways the world is created. Of how what I think I know of my own desires is only the result of being told what to feel, crave, or reject. I can't control much from my cubicle—my daily life is compacted into numbers, goals, expectations, and meetings. Maybe it's a beautifully engineered illusion that leads me to think I have choice when all I really have are predetermined options. Somewhere between isolation and delusion, I continue to log on and be told who I should be or what is important. I like to think that by crafting profiles and choosing photos I have some sway over what I see. I forget the ever-growing ripple of social influence and the reverberation of it returning. Each time it does, it brings back something new until what I put out is smoothed like sea glass—beautiful but not what I gave to the world.

· · · · ·

I CAN'T BE SURE if my affinity for *The Truman Show* existed when it was released because I can't remember where and when I first saw it. In June 1998, I'd just finished my freshman year of college and was in the throes of an identity crisis. I just know the movie exists in my head, and when I watch a snippet, a flood of thoughts come rushing in. I point at my computer and make noises of agreement at the screen because even if the feelings of being out of control are new, they are true. I will struggle with these emotions for a very long time.

Watching the clips of the film—microdosing it over a few days—is the best way to keep myself from thinking too deeply. My father recalls I've always been this way. He tells me to suspend belief when we watch television together. That just because something isn't quite right from scene to scene doesn't make the show less entertaining. He says in my childhood I'd ask if the world was real—that if we turned around, would the world behind us exist? Or I'd ask if we were just exhibits in a larger zoo being watched from above. I think of Truman and how he must have had both of these questions. When the life around him started to glitch, how it must have felt to think he was seeing the world being created or destroyed in real time.

Truman lived in perfect, blissful ignorance. He was told what to believe. What to feel. Who to love. How to exist in complete marketing harmony. But the town in which he lived was flush against him—so little room to move that he only needed to flex to shatter it. Truman needed only to be late, early, or indifferent, and the whole scheme would have shifted. It would have been suffocating if he'd truly known just how deceitful those moving around him had been. But perhaps not. The algorithm is almost seamless. Just maybe Truman would have absorbed the meddling just as we have and be happy for it.

The 1989 *Twilight Zone* episode "Special Service" gives me a glimpse of how this scenario would look. John Selig is just like Truman—an ordinary man with a standard life until the world he thinks he knows glitches. He discovers a camera behind his bathroom mirror and is suddenly thrust into making a decision he could have never seen coming. Does he stay "unaware" of the cameras and continue on like normal, or does he decide he wants the privacy of which he's been unknowingly stripped? John makes a decision that in our modern times I think many would understand. Faced with the prospect of the money, women, and charmed life being taken from him, he feels he's made a mistake by pushing for his newly discovered show to end. Thankfully, for him, it seems the powers that be lied about his show's cancellation to guide him back to the status quo. This lie allows everyone to get what they want. The network continues to make money and John gets his fame for simply being him. The head of the network tells him, "Some people are famous for being famous. You put their face on TV often enough and before you know it, they become a celebrity."

In contrast, the saddest part of *The Truman Show* wasn't the similar lies on which everything was built. And it's not how Truman was stripped from ever knowing a real family and was severed from anyone with even an inkling of sympathy for him. The true cruelty of it was the illusion. It was the bubble in which he lived and the reflection of some idyllic life that never actually was—the pressing down of a false sky and an electric sun. The meanness of it was the perfectly curated stage on which he existed and the unseen hands controlling even the most minute details. Stripped of any agency, Truman was given the totality of the trappings of the American Dream—but never allowed to wake up to see what could really be if he'd had true choice.

I spend so much of my time trying to make myself a perfectly serviceable human that I make myself less of a person.

So much time is spent trying to strip down the pieces of me in order to be the perfect everything. The perfect daughter. The perfect sister. The perfect employee. The perfect friend. I am good at none of them. What's left of the true me is a shell that fits what happened to Truman. Everything around me is false. And in my pursuit of perfection, I put myself into the same type of bubble that he was in, except in this life I am very clear it exists. I know what the bubble is constructed of; how shiny it looks in the light; and how dull it is from the inside. I live inside it. I created it. And I know exactly why I've done so. I've done so because it is easier for people to see the warped version of me behind the bubble's glass. It's easier for me to allow the roles to shift and change what's good and what's bad in my personality as much as my physical being.

In the movie, when Truman sees a tiny glimpse of reality—actors waiting for their cues behind a false wall—the world around him rearranges itself to cover up the lies. When he continues to try to see beyond the facade, he's treated as if he is crazy. The powers that be scramble to divert his attention and recurtain the gaps. I know how Truman feels seeing the veil slip—how the world sometimes seems to glitch—and I can see something isn't quite right before I'm distracted again. The powers that be lead Truman down an alternate path just so he can end up exactly where they want him. Blind and ignorant to reality. And when everything is back in proper motion, the illusion seems once again set in stone. But it isn't.

Truman's brain has cracked open and the light of truth has started to seep in. He begins to see the world for what it is—a series of advertisements, set pieces, and actors hiding their true selves for the sake of profit and exposure. In Truman's isolation experiment it was possible to build the lie that a brief interruption of the status quo could change the world. That if Truman shook the algorithm just a little, the entirety of the scheme would collapse. So, the world does what it does—forces its denizens to doubt themselves until they fall back in line.

During the upswing of the movie, a stage light falls from the "sky" above Truman's head, and there it is—a physical clue—that the world is not what it seems. We see these cues in our world too. A network goes down. A filter glitches. Corporate gaffes get blamed on rogue employees. People get recorded behaving badly. But the world always seems to smooth out the wrinkles, and it all becomes a part of the greater moving picture—turned into memes and viral videos that will later "define" a decade. During the summer of 2020, as protests roared and fires burned, a sea of black squares on Instagram told us that Black Lives Matter, but a year later all that remained of that time was lip service and the next round of causes du jour. That was our light falling from the sky, and we barely blinked.

• • • • •

CHRISTOF, THE MASTERMIND BEHIND the massive reality show in *The Truman Show*, tells Truman toward the end of the movie, "I know you better than you know yourself." In the movie, Christof is like the algorithm—always curating what's seen, felt, heard, or bought. He, just like that digital knowledge bank, convinces us an individual is the star, is so important the world revolves around that person. He makes this desirable and impossible to avoid. But in this augmented reality? The individual is just product, project, and financial energy.

Those who buck against the system are treated like pariahs and banished from the world. Truman's faux father was removed entirely from the show until he fell into step. Then and only then was he integrated back into the world. I've kind of seen this before. On TikTok, I see those stranded in the algorithm. They beg for interaction so they may find the right side of their interests. They query what they had done that led them to portions of the app where their content is assailed by what seems like archnemeses. They want to get back to the illusion of control. What is a mirage if it's not catered to your desires? In "Special Service," right after the television series is exposed, John arrives at the television station amid a throng of women shouting and clamoring for him. It's almost like he contemplates if he must give up a part of himself if this attention is worth the trade-off. He decides that it is.

Those TikTok users are asking not to be sucked into purgatory—that if they must be a part of this wave, they have the choice of where they drown. Sometimes this banishment feels like punishment. Showing even a passing interest in something off the chosen path sets off a spiral. It makes us afraid to experience something new lest our whole worldview shifts without our permission.

"We accept the reality of the world with which we are presented," Christof says when speaking about how Truman has yet to figure out the true nature of his life. And he's right. These people on TikTok who begged to find a few familiar faces and common interests know the world is not what they make. They can only exist within the construct with which they are presented, and the only real option is to make the best of it.

· · · · ·

ON A PLANE, on the way to the blaring illusion of Los Angeles, I watched *The Social Dilemma*. The film uses a fictional family, specifically a teenage boy, to showcase how the smallest of social media decisions sets off a chain reaction. Everything has a disproportionate result—nothing is ever casual.

I recognized the patterns of my social platforms swayed me once I showed even a passing interest in something and how my view of the other users around me ebbed and flowed depending on which platform, time, or day I logged on. Still, I found myself judging those people silly enough to keep falling for the mirage of their online life. Like I'd cracked some code and was too smart to fall for any of it. I wasn't the extreme user who gets the most attention or the most ridicule. Not too conservative or too liberal. I think I was the perfect storm of user. Educated with disposable income and a little too much confidence when it came to how the algorithm works. I thought I was above it all.

Yet, as soon as the plane landed, I switched away from airplane mode and waited for the satisfying ding of notification. I went to Instagram first to see who'd liked the short clip of my Converse walking in the airport. I've posted this type of video so often that people remind me to do it before each of my trips. I've influenced them in my own way. This "power" lofts me a bit higher for a moment, and I feel like I've accomplished something if only for a little while. It's in these fleeting moments I can understand the grip this control had on Christof. You can make people long for something even if they hold no real power in their actual lives. This false sense of control makes them feel a part of something, and I think it really all boils down to that. It comes from the need to feel important even if we are not truly seen. It's a longing for knowledge that we actually impact and change the world even if there is truly no balance between illusion and reality.

• • • • •

SPOILER ALERT: This is how *The Truman Show* ends.

Imagine the sky is so close Truman can flatten a hand against it. So close he can beat his palm against its matte blue until he tires and breaks into tears that are much saltier and realistic than the ocean on which he floats. Beneath his palm, he learns the sky has texture like concrete. It is hard and unforgiving—not the expected softness he could only imagine it should be. There are no actual clouds, and this sky is not real, but there it is all around him. He begins to believe the sky feels like a trap, and it is too.

Imagine all Truman knows about his life reveals itself to be a lie. Maybe there are portions of it that are actually built on the truth, but it's difficult to see beyond the haze he's always known. Truman begins to understand the world can be everything or it could be nothing. Or it could be something in between. Perhaps the pieces of it that give him the most comfort are real because at least they are the portions of his life that weren't ready made for him. Deep beneath all of the untruths Truman has started to uncover, there is at least a kernel of something organic.

Imagine how it feels for Truman to know the small slips in his sanity were not the splintering of his mind but rather a wellspring of programming and deception in service of a greater "good." That he'd been watched and manipulated from the time he was born—never away from millions of eyes. To them all he'd ever been is entertainment or a puppet on a fiber-optic string. Imagine Truman has come to these realizations when the world runs out right in front of his eyes and he's too afraid to go back from whence he came.

In the distance, far across the faux ocean and still under this false sky, there is all he's ever known. It is drifting from him until soon it will be not even a memory. It will be a scar. Truman discovers there is a door in this sky and a stairway too. This is his escape—his first real decision. Stay in the illusion or see what exists on the other side.

I Was in Love
with Jake Sisko

A week after I get to Portland for an extended writing residency I've desperately needed, my cousin asks me to visit her just outside of Seattle. I try to remember the last time I've seen her in person and come to believe it was at her father's funeral just about twenty years ago. Her dad, Daniel, was my father's half brother. I remember him—towering over everyone else I knew—behind the meat counter of Ralph's Store back home or in his uniform as a member of the local police department. I clearly remember the baby blue of his casket, and I know in my box of family photos and memories his obituary is still there among the rest that time has piled into the box.

My cousin says her boyfriend will drive the couple of hours down to pick me up, but I refuse so I find myself at the Amtrak station on a misty morning just as the sun is peeking over the horizon. The station is nearly empty but I still feel out of place. I soothe myself by pretending I am so elegant that those who stare at me are doing so because I am mysterious, magnetic. Not because I am Black and the only other face of color is an employee manning a security desk. I make it a point to nod and smile when I pass him just as the train is starting to board.

The train pulls down the track slowly—picking up speed until the mist cloaking the city now covers a lush green that could never be the same back East. All of the world is blanketed in rain and the sky stays the same dull gray between the trees. The landscape is unremarkable but oddly magical. Half reality and half fairyland. But none of what I see is interesting until the water appears. The train travels so close to it there is a sliver of nothing between where the car ends and the waves begin. The water is silvery beside the tracks, and if not for the rocking sway of the car and clank of the wheels, I'd think we were floating. I take secret videos of the expanse of ocean to avoid looking too much like a tourist. I want to belong here among the other passengers, with their noses pressed into books or staring down into screens.

I pride myself on blending into the background of the places I visit—not someone new, just someone familiar. When I travel, I often exist outside of who I really am. I stare out of windows—buses, trains, planes, ride shares, and subways—a new person equipped to handle whatever the destination may be. This is me now, trench coat casually draped open and a puff of frizzy curls pushed back from my face. A studious woman with a pen clenched between her teeth while she highlights a dog-eared page. Reading about the movie *Black Panther* and its cultural impact while leaving one of the whitest cities in the nation, half pretending I'm something I'm not.

• • • • •

WHEN WE HIT THE HALFWAY point of the trip, I am scribbling notes and highlighting pages in the book spread open by the V of my fingers. I write that I insert myself into the person I want to be like a second skin. I suppose I believe there has always been a part of me that has existed in a fantasy world. My mother says I was around two years old the first time I made letters. Scrawled across the back of an oversized studio-posed picture of me, there appears, in blue pen, *e t o G F R A*. This is not a word, but it is an understanding of where I would eventually begin to hide. Between letters and words and stories in order to make sense of the world or to build it out just as I needed and wanted it to be.

One of the earliest fantasies I can remember having is being the youngest Jackson. In this make-believe world, Michael and Janet and Rebbie were in awe of me and I was the star. Except I'd been hit by a train and all they could see of my body was one arm extending from a cardboard box serving as a hospital ICU unit. At my childhood home on Linden Avenue, before I started writing them down seriously, I created elaborate scenarios that I pushed out of my head into the quietness of my playroom, and I guess in some ways I've never stopped. Those scenarios are there as I fall asleep or daydream about being swept away into a new life, or perhaps being a new person, though the distance between how much I believe this can come true has greatly widened.

• • • • •

I ARRIVE IN TUKWILA, WASHINGTON, beneath the mist that has followed me from Portland. A small handful of us pour from the train and I text my cousin I've arrived. She pulls up in a black BMW, and the face staring back at me from the window looks like every woman I know. Twenty years have shrunken down to a singular day when she hugs me and we pull out of the parking lot. She looks so much like family that I forget the last I've seen her I was just over twenty-one. I've lived several lives since then, but there we are suspended in amber. We drive toward her home with me filling in the gaps of the decades until we settle into the thought that we are among the last of our family name. She's proud I'm in Portland to write and the next morning while we wait for my return train, she'll tell the businessman beside us about my book with light in her voice. When I start to fall asleep in her guest bedroom that evening, with *Unsolved Mysteries* flickering in the darkness, I worry about the weight of being where this branch of the family tree stops.

· · · · ·

AS MY COUSIN WEAVES in and out of traffic on the highway, I scroll Instagram and check in on my *Black Panther* fan page I founded three years before. It is a big deal for me to turn over control. Before I left Philadelphia, I'd designated a surrogate to run the page to ensure the momentum I'd built wasn't lost. I'd gained over eight thousand organic followers and a set of rules about how often and what I posted. What started out as a hobby was now more like a second job. So much so that in the planning of a nearly monthlong trip, finding someone to run the page was one of the priorities. I hadn't stopped my mail nor had I made a plan for my plants to be watered. What I knew was that the fan page part of my life was sorted.

From the time I was a child to just after the time I graduated high school, I wrote fan fiction and papered three walls of my childhood bedroom with posters ripped from *Right On!* and *Word Up!* magazines. I stacked copies of the *Source*, *XXL*, and *Slam* into plastic bins until they were too heavy to lift. Over the years, I've sunk my time and money into everything from basketball cards to jerseys, movie props, autographed memorabilia, and oddities just to say I have a piece of the things I love.

But it wasn't until the summer of 2021, when I heard a fellow writing-conference panelist mention parasocial relationships, that I could finally put a name to my actions. Think of parasocial relationships like this—unrequited love and one-sided friendships. It's those puppy love crushes and infatuations with New Kids on the Block or whichever of the Coreys you liked. Mine were with Another Bad Creation, Boyz II Men, Kris Kross, Wolfgang Bodison, and more. Think of the screaming hordes of girls waiting for the Beatles or tossing panties onto a stage. There are much more scientific definitions of these types of relationships, but I think it's better to use something concrete.

• • • • •

WHEN I WAS A CHILD, I had a year of collecting Batman comics before my interests moved to basketball and all the rookie cards my limited budget could obtain. I much preferred *Star Trek: Deep Space Nine* to any comic, and I am sure somewhere in a wayward basement box is my Jake Sisko action figure. Tucked away alongside it there should be my communicator, fan magazines, and novels. I'm pretty sure there are also the VHS tapes I faithfully popped into the VCR machine each week to capture the latest episode. I sometimes had to reuse the same VHS tapes on which I'd taped *All My Children*. Every now and again, there would be the splicing away of the screen and Pine Valley suddenly being catapulted into space before the paths uncrossed. Terrence and Olivia would join an intergalactic family, in my mind seemingly more comfortable there because at least a Black man was in charge.

Oh, but Jake!

I am just as sure that tucked away in some cobwebbed corner of my mind is still the possibility of being launched to the edge of a wormhole, where I'd gaze out of a portal window beside a lanky boy trying to adjust to the loss of his mother and the uprooting of his life. No matter the beige and brown bodysuit or the lanky undulation of his gait, he was the starbound boy of my dreams. If only there had been a way to press the shiny reflection of the replica of the show's communication device on my chest and hear more than that duplication of television technology. How my heart would have soared at the sound of his voice breaking into manhood as the seasons passed and his body stretched upward.

Maybe I could have been one of the dabo girls who ran the games in Quark's space casino or the shy daughter of one of the crew. Maybe Jake and I would have met in Keiko O'Brien's classroom the day Jake found his way off the promenade and behind a desk. However the meeting would have unfolded would've been of no matter. Fantasies with my television crush always ended the same. With Jake Sisko in love with me and me in love with him. And I suppose this sci-fi love opened up the possibilities of a quiet girl being the object of affection. All I had to do was just wish hard enough, or just maybe if I stood still and projected my desires onto a screen, I could walk onto the set of the life of my choosing.

The night the show debuted, I pressed my fingertips against the label strip of a tape and applied pressure until there was the click of the reel accepting my offering In my messy, oddly angled script I'd written *Deep Space Nine 01/03/1993*. Outside, far from outer space and even further from Jake, were the crickets and quiet of small-town Ohio. Inside me were the beginnings of fandom fires I'd add fuel to with each fanfic, purchase, and episode. One thing has always been true no matter my obsession. Give me a place to belong and I will give you my all.

However, by 2018, I'd fallen away from my years-long lop-sided love affair with Jake and all that came with him. From time to time, I'd moved on to other minor hyperfixations, but between the time I graduated from high school and my late thirties I'd lost all connection to fandom. What had once been such a massive part of my life had dwindled down to nothing. No more *Deep Space Nine*, *New York Undercover*, or *The Practice*. My love of the Orlando Magic's Anfernee Hardaway was over as was my crush on Corliss Williamson, the star of the Arkansas Razorbacks basketball team during my high school years.

When Marvel launched their cinematic universe in 2008, I made it a point to watch most of the movies even if I was less than enthused by some of the offerings. If I'm nothing else, I am committed. When the release of *Black Panther* was announced, it seemed only natural for me to watch the movie for the most basic of reasons. Black people. Black actors and a Black director with a large budget via a major studio. I thought if we didn't show up then that was it. No more blockbusters. We would have proven the industry right: They don't show up so there's no need to make art for them. I bought a ticket and went about my business waiting for February 2018 to roll around, until a grad school friend called and told me about an event a Black sci-fi group was having for the premiere. Across the news leading up to the film, there'd been a fever pitch of excitement building. Twitter threads of what people planned to wear, the joy of children being gifted tickets, and a collective enthusiasm because this movie was for us. We can recite the studies and statistics about representation, but to feel it is a whole other beast. This excitement was pride and possibility sitting squarely in front of you, and for some of us we were feeling it for the very first time.

This sci-fi group had rented out a theater for the release, and there would be cosplay, gift bags, trivia, and an afterparty at a Black-owned comic shop. That was all it took. I exchanged one ticket for the other, logged on to Etsy, bought a Wu-Tang-inspired Wakanda sweatshirt, and waited. That theater, with nearly every seat filled, was nearly 100 percent Black. Likely two hundred people in all manner of dress, Dora Milaje warriors standing with spears tall, and nearly every single one of us brimming and bursting with anticipation for the very first scene. It was glorious. Between the lights going down and when they came back up, I transported like I had as a child. I was in Wakanda—a newly minted member of the Jabari tribe. And when I went home that afternoon, just before a heavy snow started to blanket the city, I knew I needed to seek out people just as moved as me.

· · · · ·

AFTER *BLACK PANTHER,* when I picked up writing fan fiction for the first time since those early Jake Sisko days, I was ashamed. *Too old,* I told myself. *Too weird too.* What kind of middle-aged woman uses a fictional world as escapism? I chastised and questioned and nearly stopped myself from exploring what I wanted and needed. It was like all those middle and high school years of being so enthusiastic about my fandom interests didn't exist. All I saw was me in the present day when I was supposed to be serious about life and leaving behind childish things. But it was so much fun! It was like recapturing a little bit of that premiere magic, but this time I knew everyone around me was feeling the magic too and had committed to spending their free time retrofitting the world Marvel had given us. I often wonder if what I love so much about *Black Panther*, which premiered over four years ago, is the world that actually was in the movie or the enhanced ones the fans created.

What is true is that no matter my reason for going to see the film, shortly after my third viewing I started writing. I wrote hundreds of thousands of words of fanfic, bought the collectibles, and started a fan page for a singular, simple reason. It was the one thing in my life that I had zero expectations for. I know it seems like being in a parasocial relationship is the opposite of this fan page. That you are trying your best to be noticed or scooped up from the masses into some dream life, either romantic or platonic, with the apple of your eye. Perhaps when I was younger that was the goal, but the older woman who came back to fandom after twenty-plus years just wanted something for herself. A place to pin her desires and hopes and wishes on a person and a place that had zero chance of reciprocating.

This new connection to fanfic meant I had the ability to write myself into the story and see who I wanted to be and how I wished to be treated. And fandom is safe for me. I can't truly be let down if nothing is real. So I let myself get lost in it, and at some point I stopped separating my "real" writing from my fanfics. I decorated my desk with Funkos and indulged in every bit of the fandom whenever and however I liked. I started talking openly about how at times the stories I posted were the only way I kept writing, and I did my best to make all of this a legitimate part of my everyday life. It was nothing for me to scroll eBay for new additions to my collection or to take requests for new stories. I enjoyed the camaraderie I had with the other fans who were so invested in the film and its characters they were willing to create their own makeshift tribe across the cyber distance.

But after about a year of writing fics I received an angry message from a fellow fandom member who used my age as one of her insults, and all of those initial fears I'd had seemed to make sense. She thought all I wanted was my ass kissed because of the platform I'd built. She thought I was a mean girl. Cliquish. That I wasn't supportive of other writers. I could wax poetic about how easily we can tear each other down behind the veil of the internet or how what we see as shared is only a tiny fraction of our lives beyond the profiles. How you can't be all things to all people all of the time. But none of that matters when the vitriol is directed at you. The instinct is to prove the person wrong, to say "See! I am a good person!" and rattle off all of the reasons why you are. And after my initial shock, that is just what I did. It felt good when others jumped to my defense too. Yet, that message stuck with me. I carried it that entire day and into the night. She'd been so insistent to make sure I got it; she'd sent the exact message twice.

If that person wanted to hurt me, she most certainly did. She typed "imagine being in your 30s obsessing over a man who will never want you" about my love for M'Baku and the actor who played him, and all the joy I felt in finding a community amid the writers and fans of *Black Panther* sank to the bottom of my stomach. It was difficult to understand how age made me less able to like a thing, that somehow my need to escape no longer mattered. I thought, before I became angry, wasn't this the time I needed to escape most? Buried under the pressure of social expectation, a career, and the looming grays on the horizon, didn't it make sense to craft stories and pretend behind a username in a fictional world?

There is a post that floats about Tumblr. To paraphrase, women are often expected to put away their hobbies once they hit a certain age. There is no grace for us. No chance to have a singular measure of joy not connected to the service of others. That message on my fan page sucked the air from my body that morning I read it. Elana Dykewomon writes in "Notes for a Magazine," "Almost every woman I have ever met has a secret belief that she is just on the edge of madness, that there is some deep crazy part within her that she must be on guard constantly against 'losing control' of her temper, of her appetite, of her sexuality, of her feelings, of her ambition, of her secret fantasies, of her mind." Before I read the message on the fan page, there was already a tenuous relationship between my fandom and my "real" life. I exposed some of my joy to the world outside of my love for *Black Panther,* but so much of it I kept hidden lest I be judged as crazy. I tried to coddle myself by being reminded of generations of white men head over heels with Star Wars. Of Disney adults and of Harry Potter parents who sort their children into houses. I kept circling back to how massive Comic-Con is and how unfair it is to strip the feeling of escape, of belonging, from someone when you are engaged in the exact same activity.

At the crux of any fandom is the truth that it is both a reflection and a community. Even if the pseudo intimacy to our favorite characters, actors, or musicians is removed, there is still a fundamental idea among fans that we are moved by this particular thing, and this feeling of being moved extends a sense of community and understanding. When that rug is pulled from under you, it is easy to feel as if you belong nowhere. The world tends to react to these activities with either amusement or ridicule. To feel the same reaction from within an insular group is heartbreaking.

• • • • •

ON THE RAINY TRAIN RIDE between Portland and Tukwila I devoured an essay by Claudia Bucciferro. In "The Symbolic, the Real, and the Ladies of Wakanda" she writes, "Many high-achieving women attest to the idea that the fire that moves us to pursue our dreams is often kindled by a story that lights up our imagination. When we happen to be surrounded by realities that are difficult or grim, this matters even more: oppressive circumstances may compel some to 'escape' into a fantasy, yet if this fantasy can be turned into an opportunity to refuel and re-engage with conceptual possibilities, it can bear fruit."[12]

This is true. When I came back to fandom and developed parasocial relationships with a few favorite characters, these relationships became a new anchor point for my life. While I was utterly burned out by work and the desire to develop a viable writing career, my immersion into this world kept my fingers moving and my imagination engaged. It didn't matter

---

12 Howard, Sheena C., and Claudia Bucciferro. "The Symbolic, the Real, and the Ladies of Wakanda." In *Why Wakanda Matters: What Black Panther Reveals about Psychology, Identity, and Communication*, edited by Sheena C. Howard, 17–33. Dallas: BenBella Books, 2021.

if I was writing about the Jabarl hinterlands or the heart of
Birnin Zana. It all served to reignite a part of me that had once
flourished.

Outside of these still-evolving thoughts, I find it difficult to
pin down why my obsessions matter to me and how it feels to
hide them or feel judged because of them. I guess this difficulty
has something to do with my seeking a place to belong, to feel
desirable, to find out that maybe I *am* a little bit special. Who
wouldn't want to be Y/N[13] garnering the love of powerful men
and the respect of those in her chosen field and adventuring
across the world all the while being confident, intelligent, and
desired? Who wouldn't want to be understood and uplifted by
like-minded fans who sometimes cheer you on when no one
else does?

Perhaps creating a new world and a series of fictional
women-to-be is a survival tactic. A way to keep a pulse on
the innocence of what I thought life could be. If I think this
way, I am always the best version of myself. Smart and beautiful and worldly—fully competent to take over the spaces I've
always wanted to occupy. Maybe this return to the fictional
world shows me that this life is aspirational much more than it
is fantasy. Here I am: a highly educated, gainfully employed,
independent woman who lives a life most would deem something great. But this is not enough. I am not refined nor sexy
nor bright enough to draw the attention of the world. I will
never be swept into the arms of a powerful man and given the
world on a silver platter. What I tend to forget is there are tiers
to these fantasies—an entry point and a really little chance of

---

13   Y/N, aka Your Name, is an acronym commonly used in reader-insert
fan fiction stories.

escape as long as there are any ties left to this ghostly world. If I am one layer of this fantasy, what is above? What, exactly, am I trying to gain? When will it ever be enough? I don't think it ever will be. The trouble in setting yourself into these worlds is that the highs can often be just as rewarding as the downfalls are dangerous.

· · · · ·

MY COUSIN TAKES ME TO the Space Needle and we take pictures at the base—small dots against the gray sky. At the ticket window we stand behind a family of eight turned away for having the wrong COVID-19 test results. My cousin read online that as long as the capacity of a place is under five hundred, you don't need results or a vaccination card. The man behind the glass proves this is not true. She doesn't have either so she's refused entry. I say I've come cross-country, and to Washington for the first time, and wonder if she'd mind me going alone. I buy the ticket with a promise to meet her in the gift shop in an hour or less. An elevator of us tourists cram in and rocket into the sky.

At the top of the tower, the glass floor rotates beneath me and I am hesitant to place my full weight on it. I totter onto it, wait a moment, then totter some more until at least the entirety of my feet are there. All it will take is one full step backward toward the safety of the carpet. The view below is dizzying. The world seems so small but still so dangerous. I know what's below me—the concrete at the base of the tower, other tourists, a fountain jutting toward the sky before the rest of the landscape flattens and pitches between residential and business buildings. I know this floor is safe, or else the lot of us would not be allowed to step onto this disc or out onto the Space

Needle's rim. I FaceTime my father from the top with the sweep of the ocean and coast behind me as I complete my own rotation. An older couple giggles over my shoulder as I shout an explanation about why I am alone. The woman nods like she understands my decision. It is hard for my father to hear me, but I keep talking—happy to share this sliver of frightened joy. He prods me to step closer to the edge and I flip the camera so it looks as if he is leaning nearer the plates of glass separating me from a ghastly death.

When I swing my eyes straight ahead, there is the city stretched out. From here the world is what I make it. I make it devoid of people even if I can see the dots of movement below. Likely cars, but still occupied by humans. This is the world waiting to be made. I am used to populating my head with stories, with relationships, with new versions of myself. So much so that on the swift elevator ride down, I think there has been a metamorphosis. I have been changed. I step into the gift shop yet another version of myself—one who can't quite place her finger on why gazing out and over a city makes her feel as if she has accomplished something. Perhaps it is the conquering of fear that is the difference between this new version and the old, of handing over a part of myself to see how it can be transformed. I tuck this woman deep inside me with the rest of myself as my cousin and I make our way back to her car.

· · · · ·

ON THE TRAIN RIDE DOWN from Portland, I'd underlined and scribbled in the margins of my book. There were too many points that made sense—that connected to how I feel and perhaps why I operate the way I do. Most of the ideas kept circling back to the same theme—that the threads between us and our hyperfixations are about what could be or what we want to be. The foundational reasons for these feelings may vary widely, but I can't help thinking that is the crux of it. Perhaps it is the thrill of an alternate life that makes these types of fixations so intoxicating. The glimpse of seemingly anything you could ever want to bring you peace, love, wealth, or fame is right there within your grasp. You just need to be noticed and pulled through the wormhole or out of the crowd.

I can imagine there are my own deep-seated reasons I need to escape from, or reconceptualize, my life, but maybe these reasons are the continuation of my being a lonely child and now an overwhelmed adult. But one thing has always been the case: I've never wanted to be anyone other than myself. What I wanted more than anything was to be a better version of me. Sometimes she was darker or lighter. Thinner or curvier. Smarter or more popular. But she was always me. When I write fan fiction, it is an escape into the blank slate I see in my mind. There I can lay out the pieces on the surface before me and shuffle them until just what I want appears.

I often find myself writing bits of me into my fics. The women, who are either reader inserts or original characters, all share many of the same traits I have. They are intelligent and accomplished. They are independent and successful in their chosen paths and can take care of themselves. But the purpose these fantasies serve is to allow each of the women to put down the stress of the world or be appreciated just as they are or to be noticed and loved. It's not necessarily about a man sweeping in and doing much of anything. It's about the option to have it happen and being the master of just how it occurs. Depending on the particular stressors of my life, these fantasy worlds can stretch a single one-shot story or chapters building upon each other until I finally feel satisfied. And if others can relate and come along for the ride? All the better. At least we aren't alone.

But when I think of these fictional women, I get an inkling that I, their creator, am in some ways in a parasocial relationship with them. Or am I really in one with myself? Zora Neale Hurston did say gods behave like the people who created them, right? I go down the rabbit hole. What if this is true? That the deeper we dive into fandom we become enamored by these alternate versions of ourselves. The ones more popular, seemingly more talented, more appreciated by people we believe truly see us. And I suppose this is a blessing and a curse. When Bucciferro writes later in that same essay, "We also want to be able to project our own identities, as individuals and as a people, into an imagined universe, and see not our current limitations, but fresh horizons and new possibilities,"[14] I find it must be true. But is there harm in this? Is there harm in being fascinated by a version of yourself molded by your own hand in the manner you saw fit? There is. Because that person you mold is aspirational. It doesn't mean they could never be, but at some point in all the fantasies you must come back through the looking glass.

When we pass over our hearts and minds to public figures in parasocial relationships, most of us are on the other side of this glass. Maybe our noses and palms are pressed to it. Some of us may tap it or test its strength. And a few may even crash through it and lose all reason. But when it's you falling in love with an aspirational version of yourself it is hard to know where the line between confidence and delusion is crossed. It is so easy

---

14 Howard and Bucciferro, "The Symbolic, the Real, and the Ladies of Wakanda."

to create a false version of ourselves now, even if there is no ill intent. We can curate away the bad decisions and rotten parts of us and become the celebrity version of ourselves—touchable but still very far away. I think about this often. Who I am in the dark versus who I am in the light and just how far apart are the two? I now feel there is some greater reason I float so easily between fantasy and reality, as if I'm always waiting for a more bombastic life to truly come bubbling up to the surface.

I think I, and so many who grew up in Gen X and beyond, understand how it feels to live parallel lives. To sometimes be some other version of yourself ghosting just behind the surface of your flesh. And how sometimes the disconnection that comes from escapism makes it nearly impossible to come back. And those who also understand that the physical form can actually be the trap—the true place where you aren't properly fastened to the world. I think these escapes, as fun as they may be, lead us down a rabbit hole. We use manipulation as acceptance—stepping further away from the kernel of ourselves that's still true.

The next morning, on a different train headed back to Portland, the ocean view is now across the aisle because I've chosen my seat poorly. Looking at the water sliding by for too long makes my neck burn and ache, so I'm forced to look away. I've lost interest in my book, but I've jotted down a note that makes me think. In similar, more refined handwriting from those used on the *Deep Space Nine* tapes, it says "depersonalization in order to be filled back up." Maybe that is what I've been doing all these years—pulling away pieces of myself, giving them away to my interests to see what comes back, then deciding what of it is better than what was before.

Deprivation

The Groupon advertisement said these sensory-deprivation sessions relax the mind. They start by placing you at square one—stripped all the way down to your skin. A session starts with a shower in which the dirt and grime of the world is scrubbed and shampooed away. Next you step into the tank. It's warmed to the surface temperature of human skin and has about one thousand pounds of Epsom salt dissolved into 220 gallons of clean water. The pods are nine times saltier than the ocean and everybody floats. When you've settled, now acclimated to the soft neon glow and atmospheric music inside the pod, press the button to turn off the lights. Stop the music. Close the cover. Float.

I try imagining I am drifting in the middle of the Dead Sea, under a starless sky, without the means to stop myself from floating away from the shore. When I stretch my arms, widely enough to pull the muscles between my shoulder blades, I feel nothing. The sensory deprivation tank doesn't close in around me. It gets bigger and bigger until I am not sure where the water ends. I keep wiggling my fingers while thinking eventually they will touch something, anything, that will pull me back from the edge of panic. There is nothing to see in the blackness, no place to hold on to. There is only me trying to get free.

The actual Dead Sea is dying—falling into a series of sinkholes and evaporating into nothingness. Environmentalists watch for levels that indicate if soon the sea may be no more. The sinkholes have started to swallow buildings, fields, and roads and could easily swallow a human. The holes can suck a person into the lowest land point on earth, dropping them into abyss until maybe one day the salted shell of their bones finds its way back to the surface. A trolley, which transports tourists closer to the touch of water, has to extend its tracks as each year goes by because everything is receding. This will put more and more distance between human and sea until the buildings are just glimmers on the horizon. This extension adds to the great mystery of the disappearing sea because the connection between the world and the water seems severed. Solid ground continues to drown in what's left, but everyone still floats.

There are plans being discussed to fortify the Dead Sea and stabilize it before it is too late—plans to bring it back to life. The hope is that by easing the amount of water diverted by Israel and Jordan the sea can rise once again. It is nearly impossible to comprehend how a sea disappears. It is not an ocean, but it is still bigger than my imagination. Many things have disappeared in our lifetimes, but this seems like too much. We as a species have driven flora, fauna, and ozone from the earth for the sake of our own comfort. But where does a sea go? Will it rain down suddenly from the sky when we least expect it? Will we drown when the weight of it splashes from the heavens? Will it find a home in another sea—raising the levels until even more land disappears? These are the kinds of things that keep me up at night—a sea starting to disconnect from the world and wondering why this matters to me in the center of Philadelphia.

In the tank, I mull over the word *deprivation*. How it ends softly at the purse of my lips and what it means. *An act or instance of withholding or taking something away from someone or something.* I am withholding the weight of my body. I have taken away my sight. I am trying to forget the pressure of being. The water holds me aloft. It settles in the dip of my back and around the flare of my hips. I make angels in the ripple of it—slowly up and slowly down until the action of it begins to soothe me. I stop searching for the wall if only for a moment.

These sessions are supposed to allow you to disconnect from your troubles and reset. Like a baby coming into the world. Tabula rasa. Blank slate. A hard reboot. Some reviews laud these capsules of salted water as wombs. Perhaps a method to bring the floater back to long forgotten feelings of tranquility before being pushed out into noise and light. A reset. This is my third birth since 1978. I was premature then, and in the too still quiet of the tank I am thinking I wish for this gestation to be truncated too. I shimmy in the salty water, lapping the liquid over my naked skin and against the enclosure like a trapped fish.

I try to relax and expand my limbs until I'm splayed and nude in the tank. It doesn't help. This darkness is odd. I can still see beyond it, and it feels like I am tumbling toward the unknown. It feels as if in the endless black of it, there are things waiting. Maybe this is too much for me to handle. During my first float, the pod's soft neon glow helped me ease the descent into deprivation. It was smaller, more intimate. I was able to bump against the side that time. A foot, a shoulder, or my head, depending on how my body had twisted in the water. It was a semidetachment. Simply a pause before the world came back in. Today, the pod is nearly as large as the room in which it sits. Five and a half feet wide. Nine feet tall. Six and a half feet long. Being in this pod is like I am lost in the universe with little chance to make it back to something solid beneath me.

The more I concentrate on the darkness in the floatation tank around me, the more it seems psychedelic. Like a blacklight poster, matte velvet beneath fingers, full of orange, green, yellow, and blue. The Ganzfeld effect says as you take away senses, the others are heightened and hallucinations can occur—like a kaleidoscope you can't look away from. The brain tries to fill in the gaps and creates neural noise that can lead to altered states of consciousness. This makes sense because in the tank all is black and my brain is forcing me to see what is not there. Reality is getting further away—shimmering on the horizon of consciousness and sucking me deeper into an abyss. Just as the Dead Sea swallows the land and then the land swallows what's left, I've become ungrounded. I'm starting to believe the mirage.

The tank's darkness swirls and builds when I try to push it back into the familiar inkiness that lines my bedroom each night. This isn't much different. It is heavy in my mind, and I can't escape it no matter what comfort I give myself in knowing I can end this at any time. I simply need to sit up and plant myself to the bottom of the tank ten inches down, and this is all over. I stretch again, needing to touch the wall to ground myself, but the tank feels like it has exploded away from reality, and no matter how hard I try I can't skim my fingers across anything solid. Even my skin doesn't feel real. It's too slick, and each touch slides off my body like I'm waterproof.

The heartbeat in my ears is amplified by the plugs keeping the water out. The whoosh lulls me enough for my mind to wander.

I move my consciousness to Atlanta and the blue dark of the Georgia Aquarium. I remember the gentle wave of jellyfish and how I failed at convincing myself to stroke the rays breaking the surface of the touch pool. I could only imagine the blur of the animal rising out of the water and puncturing the soft spot at the crux of my shoulder and neck. How the water would stain pink until then it was red. This is irrationality talking, sloshing around in my brain because even sensory deprivation cannot shut it down.

Perhaps what is waiting on the other side of the blackness is actual life—a life that requires me to be present and not in the gauzy moments of my social media or the brightness of a phone. This life would force me to hold fast to the small occurrences. To not tweet or post about them but to rather hold on to a secret joy. To know that all is not up for consumption. Some things are just meant to be lived.

In the tank, I long for the glowing comfort of my phone and the smooth ache of my thumb muscle stretching to tap the screen. There is so much fear. The terror of missing out. Feast or famine and lost opportunities. My mind, still fighting this reset, knows the screen flickers with notifications. I've yet to figure out how to cull my need for instant response and easy access. The notifications appear. The notifications demand my attention. I fall in line. My phone is just outside the tank, placed atop my neatly folded clothes. It is nearly impossible to stop myself from using this need for my phone as an excuse to cut this float short. I get this anxious feeling in the base of my spine, and it slinks its way up my body until it's settled so deeply in my brain the choice seems already made for me.

The bartender at my hotel the weekend I visited the aquarium called me an outlier. He watched me scribble notes into a hardback journal spread open like a broken bird on the bar top. I looked up at him, then stuffed another blue crab–deviled egg into my mouth and asked him what he meant. He said, "Most people come to the bar and tap away at their phones, but here you are writing in pen and ink on actual paper. You're an outlier." I am a liar. One whose phone was simply tucked into her pocket while she pretended to be deep and mysterious in a new city.

But when the phone is not in my hand, I feel unmoored. It's kind of like the Dead Sea being brilliant blue and beautiful to the eye. But it's not really a sea. It is a lake under a grand illusion. Like me pretending that everything outside the purview of the camera lens isn't falling apart. In the tank, the disconnect from these connections, and my dependency on the escape they provide, almost weighs me down. I need to keep floating. I need to get above the surface. How many minutes have passed now? Maybe the wrinkles in the pads of my fingers will tell me and I can count down to when I can push back into the artificial light of the float parlor and the comforting glow of a screen. My fingers tell me nothing. The ache in my thumb still hums. I try to pull my mind back to something weightless. Something beyond intrusive thoughts. Something beyond the screen I cannot see.

I try stretching my arms again, hoping this time the gentle undulation of the water beneath me has pushed me closer to a wall, but it hasn't. There is panic starting to settle into my heart, and I try to remember there is no one here but me. There is nothing but water and thought and quiet. There lies the fear. My phone makes it easy to forget what I am afraid of. Dying alone. Being a failure. Not leaving a legacy. If I can stay connected, I can perhaps have all these things. When I sync my breathing to the lap of the water, my heart finally settles. Two beats, then a wave. Two beats, then a wave until before I know it ninety minutes are over and the room comes to life in a gentle rise of music. I think the disconnection of consciousness from my body has failed, but I will try again and hope the next time I am successful.

I scramble to emerge from the tank before it begins to filter the traces of me from the water. Before it removes the bits of me left behind until everything is once again blank. When I step back into the light, I check my notifications nude—ignoring the film of drying salt on my skin that turns me ghostly white. I am a specter trying to return to flesh, and the ground is now solid beneath my feet.

PART THREE
Coming Home

RECOMMENDED LISTENING

"You Will Rise" by Sweetback

"Umi Says" by Mos Def

"Sing About Me, I'm Dying of Thirst"
by Kendrick Lamar

You Have the Right to Remain Silent

An officer's voice unfurls from his throat and echoes out between the rain and the engine of the car. He must know the power of language and how it barrels from his chest, pools itself between his lips before it breaks the world around it. There must be an understanding of how all this works because this is how it begins. It's like time slows down and I can hear every single inhale and exhale as he shouts the words again. "Throw the keys out of the car! Put your hands on the dash! Do! Not! Move!"

In linguistics the mouth matters. The throat matters as much as the lips and the tongue. These things determine how words are formed, tells the listener the intention behind them. Fricatives, the sounds forming vibrations against the vocal cords like trembling, move the air into what we hear. *Hard. Ahead. Save. Rise.* We find these words between the roofs of our mouths, between our teeth and lips, in the lengths of our throats, and against, again, the tongue. We siphon in the air, then let it back into the atmosphere changed.

I curl my fingers against the burgundy dashboard, but the sweat on my palms and the shaking of my arms makes it hard to keep still. I'm afraid. If my arms, vibrating like words still in the throat, could talk, they would say *I am not a threat.* They would rise until my fingertips skimmed the headliner, and behind us, halfway out his car and shielded behind his cruiser door, the officer could see my hands were empty. I follow directions, not willing to shift my eyes to my best friend beside me. I am unwilling to speak. Perhaps I have forgotten how. We stare straight ahead into the rain. The drops plop and splash on the white paint, the cracked asphalt of the road ahead, and my forearm nearest the open window. There is a breeze, cool and full of the rustle of leaves.

Fricatives are only air. They are only breath finding its way among the structure of our mouths once we know where to place all the parts. Imagine, at the beginning of language, how this was once simply breathing until someone pushed beyond. Breathing is instinct. Fight or flight is instinct. I forget how to breathe until my chest burns, until I'm choking back tears as three more sirens sound across the distance. One behind. Two beside. One ahead. *Four* is a fricative. It leaves me breathless.

Backup, which crested over the hill like the calvary, does not save us. They bring more guns and the same words even after the keys have splattered with the rain on the street. The officer appears then, ruddy and dark haired, with a pistol in his hand. He is still standing in the power of his words, still shouting for us to remain unmoving. Another officer pulls me out of the car and into the rain. He presses my palms flat on the still warm hood, spreads my legs wide. The wash of rain and hands knocks me silent. It takes the breath from my throat.

I try breathing now, as slow and steady as I can in the cold rain with two guns trained. The officer finishes his search and leaves me palms down, eyes down, with instructions not to move. There is no room beside me for another body; the spread of my arms is too wide as are my legs. In the loud officer's car, there is still language. There is dryness and whiteness and whispers. This is where he takes my friend. She is delicate. Bright green eyes, a smattering of freckles, and waves of hair skimming her tiny body. *Queen* is a plosive.

Language directs us how to act. It moves our limbs as much as our mouths. It fires our brains into action. It surrounds us as much as it shelters us. I know when to speak. I know when to forget. I forget now and let sound be rain and laughter and small talk. Silence lets me piece together the story.

To him, the voice from the beginning, we have been evasive. Defied his commands to pull onto the gravelly shoulder. I remember the truth. I remember the first sight of the light bar in the rearview mirror, the steady pace of my friend's foot on the gas pedal. We waited for him to pass. Then waited for the sirens and lights. He rolled closer. Close enough we drifted from the road and beyond the white stripe to let him pass. Then lights, sirens, the beginnings of language leaving my body. She threw the keys out of the car and gripped the wheel until her fingers looked like ghosts.

Affricatives are a bridge. They stop the air and blend into words between the teeth, tongue, and lips. *Choose. Jet. Catch.* They can be voiced or voiceless. Voiced affricatives vibrate as the sound is produced, welling up and out of the body like a spring. *Agenda* is an example. A voiceless affricative needs only air. Like *gesture*. The beckoning of fingers tells me I can remove my palms and release the tension from my spine.

Tells me to linger in the rain while being pulled back to the beginnings of language, trying to move air into words. The voiceless *question* too.

Dispatch. The voice between the crackles put a description into his ear. Tells him of a robbery from which a car had fled. Had I a voice, had I less fear, I would question the validity of a duo of high school girls in a white Buick Century casually driving the speed limit down a country road matching the culprits. He does not tell us who he is looking for. We only know that he is looking.

The loud officer wants to catch me in a lie so he starts by not speaking with me. He asks my friend instead.

The common grammar is at play here. Ascribing character to words to build a picture you want to see. It is an accepted foundation that says words do not only convey meaning, they are a way to reinforce meaning. Words have power. Of manifestation and sway and accusation. Of conviction and interrogation. *Four* is a fricative. It is also the number of ways you can determine what a word can mean.

Control the sound and meter to put emphasis on what's important. Who *is* she? *How* do you know her? Are *you* okay?

Control the speed of vowels and constants and the disposition of pauses. You know . . . you can tell me if you don't feel safe. This is your . . . friend?

Choose sounds and group them so they are euphonious or cacophonous to the ear. The singsong way his questions perk up at the end like friendship. All you have to do is tell me the truth, right?!

Choose words that suggest their meaning. Except I'm still trying to find my language when the two of us find ourselves back inside the car, seat belts buckled, with an escort to the edge of town. Maybe escort means something else. A caravan. A convoy. An usher away from where I don't belong.

Again, academia tells us what we need to know. Culture refers to the process by which some particular kinds of learning are spread from person to person and minds become coordinated into shared patterns. This is culture at the edge of a town, a small cadre of officers just across a line. A friendly warning about returning. Still bank robbers on the loose. The right to remain silent about it all. The right to breathe again when the vibrations and the breath return.

Distillation

We are the only car in the drive-thru convenience store. This is a place where you can, from the comfort of your vehicle, purchase what you need. Chips and candy. Cigarettes and lottery. Vodka and beer. We are here on a quick run—nothing more and nothing less. So, it was not a surprise she said nothing of my fancy European suv when we climbed into it a few minutes ago—just ignored its insistent dinging when she forgot the seatbelt. She didn't seem to care about the heated leather seats, the bright navigation screen, or the matching black rims and tint. The bar attached to this curve of building is of no interest either. Our destination is in and out with no need to leave the warmth of this space. My faux big-city success means nothing during this weekend visit.

It is January cold and I can see my breath as the window slides down. The clerk who approaches the driver's side worries me. The camo jacket, the beard, the whiteness of his skin in the middle of Ohio is not unusual. But we are nearly three weeks removed from insurrection and I don't know if he is an enemy or simply indifferent. But he knows her. From beside me she leans over and he asks if she wants a pint or a fifth. This must be ritual. This must be daily. I don't hear her, but he returns with a fifth and she balances a twenty toward me in fingers capped by long, curling, natural nails. I pass her the bottle in exchange for the money. Four dollars and sixty cents is the price for an icy-cold plastic bottle of vodka.

Imagine the 16.7 million gallons of spirits sold in Ohio in 2020.[15] How it would crest over the landscape creating joy and sorrow in its wake. How it would wash away foundations and build a slope of bottles clattering across generations. I think of the liquor as slow—a crawl of destruction propped upon tradition and necessity. Whether it be long factory days and broken bodies scratching toward an American dream or keeping up middle-class appearances behind crystal glasses, it all goes down the same.

She relaxes back into the seat, the change crumpled in her hand and we drift toward the mouth of the drive-thru. I can't see her face fully, but I catch a glimpse of her eyes in the side-view mirror. An hour ago, before this impromptu store run, she cried when she recognized mine behind the mask. Her eyes remind me of my favorite picture—a closeup of my grandmother peering through her fingers. The family eyes, equal parts round and almond, sometimes hold a yellow tint from alcohol. If I place a scent to some of these memories, they would smell like gin. Like quilted glasses filled with ice and Seagram's, the condensation falling down the sides like juice.

Liquor has been in my orbit since I can remember. Friends and family soaked and joyous. Angry and addicted. It's made

---

15 https://www.daytondailynews.com/news/pandemic-fueled-spirits-sales-surged-in-ohio-in-2020/QOSYRITYZZFQ7N5DHYNVALRNU4/.

me fearful of sinking too deeply into the taste of it. I can count on one hand the number of times I've lost control and let it consume me. I know the way it can creep into your days and spread like smoke until you are suffocated.

We leave a trail of exhaust behind us, bouncing a bit as we hit the potholes in the block. Across the street I can see the shell of the factory where my mother used to work. Even farther down the road is a skeleton-like playground and then a junkyard full of car parts and metal. It eventually buttresses against the rise of the steel foundry where my father spent his working years.

Above the rumble of the railroad tracks, the SUV holds steady. Its smooth ride is worth the money. The steering wheel is heated in my hands. It's pushed off the cool memory of the plastic bottle so I can pretend it no longer exists. It's an osmosis of forgetting. I loop the block back toward her house. I already know I don't want to come back inside. I always mean to visit her when I am home, but it all feels too close. Too close to loose limbs and tongues slick with liquor. Too close to secrets I'm now old enough to know. Too close to troubles I'm still pretending are manageable.

I want to take a longer way home just to see things. Maybe they will be as I remember. I doubt that will be true. On the corner, there is another shell. This one a store where the school bus let out and a rush of people could loiter inside and out. We glide past it and roll to a stop across the way from her front porch. A glance shows the indent of her fingers fogging the bottle. There is no bag to buffer it.

The two of us lean into each other, cheek to cheek, like dancing. I promise to bring her a bowl of greens from my parents' the next day. I won't. I am ashamed of this lie, but it gets me through while I watch her cross the street and linger until she is inside. The lie lets me shake off the cold from when her door opened. It gets sucked up into the heat of the seats and I pull off. I skirt another corner, and behind the chain-link fence of the city impound lot, the vehicles are twisted toward the gray sky.

I talk about alcohol as if I am removed from it. This is a half truth. The addiction of it is in my veins, so I try to temper it. I try to distill it to something I can handle. What is left of the addiction is like vapor in my hands. There is still the potential of danger, but somehow, it is easier to exist this way. It is cleaner to live in the distance I've put between me and my lineage until there is only a shot of the troubles left. What remains is smoother to swallow and better than what could be.

From here home is a straight shot. I've driven this path so many times I don't even know the names of the streets. It's just instinct and landmarks until the driveway appears. I travel a little out of my way—a short block that adds only a few seconds to the ride. It puts a bit of distance between where I was and where I'm going before arriving at the intersection where her road crosses the street that will take me home.

Superstition

I

Norma Jean Snow (March 22, 1957–December 3, 2017)

It is not until after her death I find myself struggling to find one shining memory of my godmother to latch on to. There are plenty of singular, unremarkable occurrences, and in my grief, I've convinced myself these are not enough. Conditioned to believe there should be a crater of influence, I keep gazing beyond the rest of the minute impacts. Looking for the greater how, I suppose. Where I finally find the pool of grief is in the mundane. There is no largeness to it. No heft. Only parts of my daily existence I can tie back to her.

I pray before each road trip or take-off. *Please let us make it there without any car trouble, accidents, or police* is what I say no matter the method of travel. I think this pattern of asking the universe for safe passage started with traveling mercies and the rosary hanging from the rearview mirror of my godmother's Ford Escort. She had a prayer, too, even if I no longer remember it.

When we were small, Jeanie, my godmother, took her children and me on road trips. We'd pile into that gray hatchback and pull out of the cul-de-sac sometimes unsure about just where we were headed. Sometimes it was the community center. A place where the pool chlorine smacked us in the eyes as soon as the door opened. Where countless birthdays were held before hotel parties became a thing. Juice, sheet cake, pizza, and a pool were all it took. This was where the tiles were slick beneath our feet and we waddled along the edge before slipping our bodies into the water.

Other times, it was the tennis courts. I never felt comfortable there, unathletic as I was at the time, but watching her daughter and son, Angela and Michael, was enough for me. There were those days she'd switch on the television and we'd watch match after match. Navratilova. Graf. Sampras. Agassi. This was before Venus and Serena, so Jeanie, Angela, and Michael were the only Black people I knew who played tennis. They were the only Black Catholics I knew too.

One of those times we took to the road—winding that Escort across Ohio and into Pennsylvania—awaiting a surprise she wouldn't reveal to us. Dotted along the highway, signs warned us of falling rock. It seemed the guardrails could never be enough to keep boulders from sliding down the hills and smashing our car like in a video game. We children were frightened. And in our childish thoughts somehow Angela and I came to the conclusion a blanket could protect us. We pulled the brown sheet of woolen nubs over our heads, plunged ourselves into hot darkness—tiny pinpricks of light pushing through where the fabric was threadbare. We were safe then. And when the blanket pulled back, Hershey Park grew larger on the horizon.

My godmother made me love *West Side Story*, showed me how to cry over the body of Tony each time the tape looped back to the beginning even if she loved Bernardo more. Years later, when a man I knew changed the lyrics of *Maria* to Athena, I swooned at the romance of it. I could never quite remember all of the couples were doomed from the beginning. Our time together was *Bye Bye Birdie* and *Grease*, when I had tentative crushes on Conrad Birdie and John Travolta that eventually morphed into me knowing every word even after the infatuations faded. I wrote some of my first short stories on a white word processor at her home with no white-out or correction tape. The mistakes had to stand and become a part of the greater narrative. Those stories still live in a suitcase I've carted from my childhood bedroom to a shelf on my office bookshelf hundreds of miles away.

My godmother was always sunflower seeds and bingo. A cat named Lady and a personalized bedtime story to help us sleep. *Dream I may. Dream I might. Dreamo give me good dreams tonight* warded off what was frightening in the dark. She was *Soap Digest* and Cream of Wheat that no one had perfected like her. Under her hand I learned the superstitions of bingo—the saved seats, lucky daubers, and charms to place on the cards. I watched from child to adult as she won and lost but was still generous in between. She taught me the practical magic of everyday and how sometimes it was the comfort of routine that made you feel lucky.

II

Louverta Carol Dixon (December 16, 1936–August 4, 1982)

In September 2020, when my parents come to visit me during the dragging months of the pandemic, my dad sets the broken clock on my living room wall to 11:11. He says that number followed his mother and some nights she'd have him stay awake with her just to see the bedside clock flip to the numerals. For a year now my grandmother's number has not left me. It flashes across screens, watches, and computers more than I can be comfortable with. What I know about the number is you are supposed to make a wish and hold it closely to your chest. Like blowing out birthday candles or making wishes on fallen eyelashes. During this magical sixty seconds, twice a day, you can make anything come true. I tend to close my eyes tightly when I see it, half whispering what I want to manifest just in case someone is in earshot. I do my best to keep my eyes closed for the duration because something tells me this is how it works best. I'm not sure from where this stems. It just makes sense, so when I see it, I react as the spirit moves me.

As with most things I don't fully understand, I take my curiosity to the internet and lose myself for far too long. I'm careful to avoid sites whose names seem sketchy even if I don't know which are really reputable. I'm relying on some sort of pull to lead me to the correct one. When I settle on a site, I learn 11:11 is a message from the universe you are on the right path. It means that you can manifest what you want, but the site warns me to be careful of thinking negative thoughts. This sign is about positivity and growth. Whenever you see it, you are to rest assured this means you are headed in the right direction.[16]

"She'll be watching over you now," Dad says, and I wonder if I should make an altar beneath the clock. Fresh flowers and a candle. Maybe the altar should include the four elements plus one, like the tarot reader told me to gather during a cold

---

16 https://stylecaster.com/feature/11-11-date-meaning-1063029/.

December night in New Orleans. That man told me greatness was coming and to not rest on my laurels. He told me there are ancestors walking with me and to honor them with offering. A handful of crystals, dirt, or stones for earth. Incense for fire. A shell for water. A feather for air. A candle to speak across the flame. He jotted down his directives onto a scrap of yellow lined paper passed between our fingers with the cash.

The tarot man cautioned me to look for feathers in my path. A week later there was a broken one tucked into the grass. He didn't say it had to be whole. Only that I needed to collect it in honor of the altar. The feather made me remember a stark white wing slowly sinking in an oily puddle in my old job's parking lot. How it stopped me in my tracks to see only the singular curve of feathers in my path but nothing else of the whole body. I'd wanted to look away from the pink glisten of the meat, just a flash of color at the torn edge of the feathers. Those fragments, the memory and knowledge of beauty and death, scared me then and frighten me now.

The night after my parents leave, I pray myself to sleep when I hear a creak of footsteps in the living room, convinced 11:11 has brought fruit to bear. There is no altar now. Just the dying remains of last week's flowers, and I wonder if keeping them there is disrespectful. Behind tightly closed eyes, I repeat a litany to ward against the fear. *God, please watch over me and my family. God, please watch over me and my family. God, please watch over me and my family.*

I pray myself to sleep. When I wake, the flowers beneath the clock are still dead. I debate pulling my dismantled altar back together and speaking across the flame again. I wonder if the ritual of it makes me feel and not the actual energy. Maybe it is a placebo for the soul, but it's something. The altar remains in pieces, but I wish upon ıı:ıı in the morning, then decide that my grandmother is just making her presence known and moving me down the correct path even if I'm not quite seeing the way.

I remind my father of the clock a few months later. I'm almost gleeful to tell him ıı:ıı remains. I've started to believe in magic and the possibility there is some goodness floating in my home. "I bent the arms to make them stay," he confesses, and just a little of that magic flares up, then dies like flash paper in a parlor trick. There's no smoke or real destruction. Maybe all I can really feel is the smallest of shifts in the world, kind of like the gentle way a feather hits the earth.

III

The night before my forty-third birthday, as I'm rapidly approaching my grandmother's age when she passed, I ask my parents about the superstitions and rituals of their parents. My mother grew up being told not to touch paper during a lightning storm, and my brain pushes away from the idea because I am not sure how this is a danger. I file this sliver away for future research among the other scraps in my brain. She tells me, too, the red makeup sponge stored under my bathroom sink didn't start with her, but my mimic of seeing her swipe it across her face my entire childhood was her own copying of her grandmother Victoria.

My father brings me back to his mother and builds my memory of her just as he did a year before when he set the clock to ıı:ıı. He tells me she worried she wouldn't survive her latest round of surgery. She asked for dirt to be brought to the hospital, where she tucked a pinch into her mouth, tasted and swallowed it. He says he believes this was a way to connect her to the earth or to home. I've eaten paper several times in my life. Medicine says this tendency is called pica—a body missing something vital for its survival or perhaps a mental defect. If I find this earthly connection between me and my grandmother, it is a method of grounding, of remembering from where we sprung. Between pulp and dust, we've ingested the world around us.

When I learn this, the blankness in the memories of my grandmother is still there, but at least I can now find a thread toward the woman who makes up half the man who makes up half of me. And if that common link is a mouthful of dirt, then let something grow until I am speaking her words.

Maybe it is better to stay connected to each other in the unknown or the mystical. To request a piece of something solid be absorbed into us so we can never forget from whence we came. This keeps us rooted in history and the humanness that can get lost in the modern world. It's a hands-to-the-earth practice that lets each of us be free in the not knowing. It's not ignorance, it's faith and some measure of innocence that allows us to suspend belief in our current world—a port amid the chaos.

I don't imagine my grandmother tasted much of the dirt, but she felt it. Grainy against her tongue—rough at first but smoothed out wet by the time it found her throat. And when she swallowed it, the dirt became a part of her. A taste of life she'd carry with her to the other side—a memory for her son to tell his daughter.

Upon My Return

Less than twenty-four hours after my grandmother's death, I drive seven hours across the entire length of the Pennsylvania Turnpike to go help my family grieve. Another few hours later and my oldest friend Lisa and I are eating BBQ pork rinds and raising drinks at our hometown bar. I am right back where I started. Just beyond the viaduct and across the street from the Amtrak platform—a cool night at the Cantell Elks lodge. I've only been home a handful of times since I relocated to Philadelphia, and it seems each time my homecoming is because of death or a crushing sense of longing for the familiar.

Three drinks in, we balance quarters on the Formica bar top with my father. He and Lisa do so with ease, and the coins are a steady vertical my tipsy hands cannot achieve. I keep trying and trying, but the quarters keep tottering over each other and spinning out. While I try to get a single coin to balance, my father has a row of three standing. He jokes about his skill, and I am not surprised he can do it. He is talented in many ways and the only ambidextrous person I know. To my right, a lodge brother scatters the coins my dad has balanced. The four of us rise in laughter and then again when I topple Lisa's coins. It's all-or-nothing and we choose nothing.

Someone in the thin crowd of people on a Wednesday night buys another round of drinks for the bar. This is my second shot of the night, and the Red Berry Cîroc hits me in the chest. My ears flash hot. I start to feel a little wavy. This is how I describe being in the opening stages of drunkenness. I usually motion my arms like one of those inflatable tube men welcoming customers to a car lot. That, along with the burning ears, lets me know it is time to slow down or go full throttle, depending on the situation. This situation, the death of my last grandparent, seems one in which I should drain the bottle. Because I feel guilty that in the months leading up to her death I was not there to see her in the hospital or hold her hand or help bolster the spirits of those who needed it. Because I feel guilty I was afforded the distance away from the cruelty of watching her slip away. Because I took that distance even over these feelings—only showing my face when I had properly gathered myself.

I've already had tequila and rum between vodka cocktails, so it seems full throttle is the mission of the night. I'll chalk it up to grief and nerves as I have every other time I've let myself go in this way. This isn't often. I am much more likely to swallow what I'm struggling with and compact it into my soul until once in a blue moon it comes roaring out into the world. Some of the times I've come slinking home I've wanted to hide the failures of my life. News of my engagement and subsequent marriage had been in the local paper, but I'd returned home still wearing my ring with no husband in sight. I'd come back to die quickly, then slowly, for practical reasons. I'd come back to mourn and be replenished in the square miles of this place.

Too often in the last decade I've treated these returns as a cloak to my troubles. Like some kind of elixir to take away the pain.

What is true no matter my reasons for drinking tonight, or on any other, is that mixing types of liquor is never good, but I rarely listen. As long as it's not dark, anything goes. I push two dollar bills across the bar, and a new bag of rinds comes floating down. There's little grease to soak up the tequila, the vodka, and the rum, but I am hoping there is at least a buffer between the spirits and my blood.

I'm not paying attention when Lisa disappears into the tiny parking lot where we'd stood comparing our new cars. A Land Rover for me. A Cadillac for her. This is a big deal—a long way from a Ford Tempo and a Mazda. We are the daughters of manual laborers—two small-town girls under bug-filled yellow light. Lisa's father and my mother worked decades at the same garage door opener factory. Lisa now owns a home kitty-corner from it—in the shadow of the building long since closed.

I'd watched her in the parking lot beyond the smoke of her cigarette and listened to her fill in the gaps of when we weren't speaking. Nearly two years with no words exchanged between us. Lisa was the first friend I made on my own. In the second grade we were students at Liberty Elementary in Ms. Fife's class—two years later Ms. Fife would be my fourth-grade teacher as well. I'd walked up to Lisa during class one day and asked her to be my friend. I spent the formative years after that connection riding bikes and scooters with her, sleeping over in her bedroom full of the Barbies and trinkets of a fellow only child. She was, for the vast balance of my life, my other half.

In the mess of days since our last call, her mother has passed. Her father too. My grandmother. My aunt. My cousin.

Another cousin. So much death in the span of just over a year. So many to mourn. All people we loved in the ways we tether together are gone from the world. They each left a gaping hole in a swath of deaths that seems far too large to count and shows few signs of slowing. I carry the grief of not being there when she needed me most. Three decades of friendship, and I had been a ghost. She will text me weeks after tonight that she regrets missing my grandmother's funeral. In some sad way I guess we are now even.

• • • • •

WHEN LISA RETURNS FROM the parking lot, she tells me the shot made her sick. I am swimming in my brain, not quite ill but unsteady. We are old now. How many nights when we were younger would this handful of drinks have been nothing? Soon we are standing in front of the digital jukebox reliving our high school years and those beyond. It is an odd mix—half bass and half heartbreak. We flip through the song covers and try our best to remember which ones we repeated over and over again. "Ditty" by Paperboy. "Notorious Thugs" from Biggie's *Life After Death* album. "Bitter" by Meshell Ndegeocello.

When we were young we'd ride Main Street, then State Street, then Liberty Avenue until one of us got a page and we'd scramble for the nearest pay phone. We'd lie to my little sister when she was old enough to tag along about how if she covered her ears the cussing from the music wasn't that bad. Some Fridays we'd drive over to the Canton Centre Mall to pay our pager bills and trick the pagers out with new engraved nameplates and clear cases. Then we'd go home to make our outgoing messages match our current moods. My go-to was Faith's "Soon as I Get Home." Or some weekends after school we'd head to Camelot Music to buy the tapes and CDs with the music we are now selecting from the machine attached to the wall of this bar.

Lisa shimmies when the beat drops while I pretend to shuffle through more songs for the remaining credits. I am too timid to sway even the tap of my toe outside my comfort zone. It's always been this way—me peeking out from behind my shyness basked in the light of her openness.

There is a question on one of the many forms I touch daily for my job. It asks, "Does your child play next to other children, but not with them?" It takes the parents aback sometimes and some of them answer with an unsure *yes*. I imagine them flipping through scenes of their children playing and arranging the small bodies in their memories like a diorama. *Next to and not with.* I imagine my father over at the bar watching his daughter acting out a more adult version of this question. *Does your daughter dance next to her friend but not with?*

Long before I found myself worrying about dying alone in front of a screen or about the inner workings of loneliness, I'd already been somewhat disconnected. It happened without much effort. When I was born at the tail end of 1978, a month premature, my parents were shortly beyond their twenty-first birthdays. I was born into a large extended family on both sides with copious amounts of cousins, aunts, uncles, and, for a good portion of my life, grandparents and great-grands. My parents belonged to social clubs and churches. They had lifelong friends with children, and I grew up in a small town where just about everyone was connected in some roundabout way. There was no shortage of houses to visit or people to play with, but even so I found myself hard-pressed to really connect.

The evening continues to wear on—the air filling with the clack of pool balls when a group of Eastern Stars makes their way in. My dad is a pool shark—carries a stick broken down in a case in the trunk of his car. I am surprised when Lisa and I are leaving the Elks without playing a game. Too many nights—at Mangos, or Chives, or here at the Elks—I pretended the pool stick was steady in my hands and tented my crooked fingers on the felt surface to send a ball spinning into a pocket if I was lucky. I think this is how I've navigated life. Tricking people into believing what is on the surface while struggling to hold on.

Lisa and I leave a few credits on the machine because we've run out of songs to play or we can't remember any more that give us a spark. We settle back at the bar for one last drink and make a plan to head to Sheetz for a late-night snack. It feels good to be home no matter the circumstances that bring me here. I know when we leave the parking lot, the quickest route to the brightly lit gas station will be dotted with flashing traffic lights as the town turns down for the evening. I know however this night may end, at Lisa's new home or back at my parents', I will be surrounded by people who love me.

• • • • •

SOMETIME AFTER MIDNIGHT, and already tipped over into the next day, I'm back at my parents' house still swimming in my head. The lodge brother and his wife bring a late-night repast—cakes and soda and chips to my parents' house. The lodge is several drinks in the past now, but my grandmother's death still looms over my trip. This offering is important. Sometimes it is the ritual of things that sets healing into motion. It is the muscle memory of the heart saying this is what must be done. There are promises to bring another round of food later in the morning, but this is enough. We know the ripple of this grief is felt.

The group of us sit in a jagged circle in the kitchen sharing more liquor. Since I've been gone my parents have painted it bright yellow, and even though I've known this kitchen since I was twelve, the entirety of it now looks foreign to me. Eyes are low now. Voices slurred and hushed. This round I am mixing Green Apple Ciroc with a shake of ice and a splash of lemon juice. It is bitter against my tongue. Scattered across the island in the kitchen are mason jars of moonshine and Canadian Club and the vodka bottle I am tapping with my fingertips over and over again.

Since I've been gone I have gotten good at being one person here and one person in my adopted home. Tonight, even in the thickness of death, I am softer and let myself be cared for. Each time I'm home I feel so much younger in spirit that it is jarring when I go back to the life I've chosen.

The liquor is pushing my mask away tonight. I am talking about my life in Philadelphia. The people I know and the men I date. I am coy about my successes even if I am proud. The liquor loosens my tongue enough that I reach just outside my comfort zone, and for just a few hours I feel fully me. It takes this drunken grief to unleash it.

* * * * *

IN THE MORNING, after I have shaken off the heavy sleep of too many drinks, my father and I settle into another ritual we have each time I come home. We watch shows about people living in the wilds of Alaska, homesteaders building cabins on acres of land they share with their children or people alone and afraid in the wilderness trying to win a prize. In one scene, a lone man navigates a boat in a frigid river while the narrator whispers about incoming snow and the need to get back home before the skies change even further. The boat bumps against the shore after a few tense seconds, and it is clear we are to believe this man is all alone in the wild. It is also clear he isn't. My father and I talk about the improbability of the camera shots and how nothing of this is true reality television. It is at best an approximation of what life actually is.

I understand this even if I sometimes accept these shows as entertainment. What would be more realistic, although far less marketable, would be for this man to be the focus and the sweeping shots of the wilderness secondary. A much more internal view versus an external locus of control. If what we as viewers are supposed to connect with is the heart of the matter, we are forced to pay far too much attention to the body that contains it.

Before I head home my mother will give me my grand-mother's journal. I will hold on to it for nearly five months before I am brave enough to read it. I fear there is something within the pages that will shatter my memories. Of her. Of my mother, aunts and uncles. Of the family. Of myself. When I finally read it, I learn my grandmother's brain worked like mine. The fragmented entries span decades in the slim book—beginning in 1995. It is a catalog of gatherings, food, feelings, recurring dreams, everything that makes her more than just a matriarch. It makes her a person—a whole one.

Nothing in the journal makes me think the reality on the pages is curated. One entry is what she ate for breakfast—a cup of tea, 1 toast, no butter. Another entry recounts the sleepover my mother threw for me the night before I left for college. She makes no sweeping statements or ruminations about life. As she wrote on the very first page, "To those concerned: This book is just a few recorded events or happenings in my life-time." What I came to understand as I read the handwriting that looks so much like my mother's is that what is important to record shifts over time. Sometimes it is the small things that keep you going like the tea and the toast. Others recording a dream of your late husband and how he felt so real when you woke. Or perhaps how the God you've always believed in has held you steady until the very end.

· · · · ·

LATER AFTER WATCHING TV with my dad, in the misty April rain I'll go with my mother and an uncle to the cemetery and walk the soft ground looking for our blood buried beneath our feet. We want to lay my grandmother to rest with her people, so this is important. So many of us are buried here that the funeral home worker knows just what section of the cemetery to take us to, and we point out into the gray sky about who is where and what plots are available. We say Cousin is buried over there. Great-Grandma Victoria is here. And another. And another. And another. And soon one more. When this is all settled and we are back in the quiet planning room of the office, the business of dying is on the table. There are forms in triplicate and leases and money and a conversation about sinking-headstone repair.

The rep hands the three of us pamphlets with a large check-list about what to do immediately after someone dies. I decline because in my office back in Philadelphia there is a hardbound book I bought from Amazon months ago. It lays out every-thing from passwords, account numbers, and instructions on what to do once I am gone. I've told my family not to keep my body lingering. That if it and my brain are no longer in concert, then I am no longer willing to be among the "living." Just let me go. I think I want to be cremated and perhaps scattered near water. Some people have told me this is morbid, but I think completing this book must be done. These are things I must think about if I want to minimize the sadness when I am gone. I want the book in my office to be a small grace given to those left behind. There is so much heaviness associated with grief, with laying a body to rest, that if this preplanning can make the process a little less unwieldy for my loved ones, that is a victory.

It is not until we are in this office, chatting about how there are no weekend funerals being scheduled right now due to a wash of meth overdoses and COVID-19 deaths, that I realize how much more of this death planning will be occurring and how I can no longer hide away from it. It brings me back to my thoughts about returning home. One of the first times I mentioned this, my father said I have the "Philadelphia glow" and that after the nostalgia of home wore off I may regret moving back. I think this may be true, but what is the trade-off?

To slowly, and methodically, disappear from everything I know until none of it is left. It is happening now. Houses I've known are razed into overgrown lots. People I've known are now condolence posts on Facebook. Businesses shuttered. Small things that are now wildly big in my memories filter back to me as news. The local time and temperature number took its last call a few months ago. The mall, or what was left of it, is now emptied to become a grocery store. I felt these losses deep in the fiber of my being even if they seem insignificant. Each of these tiny deaths means the world as I knew it is no more.

Months after walking the cemetery with mud sticking my tennis shoes into the sopping ground, I come across a video touching on whether or not as we get older we should move closer to home. The creator asks another about his parents and learns they are in their sixties. He posits that if the man sees them once a year until the average American life expectancy is met, there are roughly fifteen more visits before they are gone. I mull over fifteen visits. This isn't fifteen Christmases or Thanksgivings or family reunions. This is fifteen of anything if my current schedule of seeing my parents once a year stands. Fifteen random drives across the turnpike because my heart hurts with loneliness. Or a few handfuls of the train rides my parents take to hang out with me when something great has occurred in my life. I cannot fathom this. It makes my insides feel liquid. My grandmother's journal spans twenty-seven years. More than this video's calculation says I have left with my own parents. I cannot breathe when I think of this.

· · · · ·

WHEN I AM HOME I sometimes drive long routes to see what I remember. I take the slower path from place to place just to see if the map in my head still exists. I rumble across the train tracks near the American Steel Foundry, then back over the viaduct and down Noble Street and back again all the way up Liberty Avenue until I am home. Dotted along this route is all that remains of my grandmother's house. Not the one I've come to mourn but instead the one who passed before I could even remember her. Last time I was here, the checkerboard doors seemed frail, almost bowing inward, beneath the backboard that now is nothing more than a shadow without a hoop or net. I snapped a picture of it on one visit. It still sits in the folder titled *Ohio* as an inspiration and a memory that belongs more to my father than it does to me.

It is very clear to me that just because the physical spaces of the world I've always known are no longer there, the memories still remain. But this is not a comfort. For several weeks after one of our impromptu FaceTime calls, my sister and I rack our brains trying to figure out what an empty storefront in our memories could be. We know it was directly across from the eye doctor's office, kitty-corner from the Taster's Choice Cafe, and beyond the rim-and-stereo-system shop that faced State Street. That night after leaving the Elks with Lisa, while on the way to Sheetz we'd driven by the entrance of that very parking lot, and the memory of the store hadn't even crossed my mind. I could have seen it then with the ghost of the marquee letters perhaps still legible if I'd given it enough effort.

Instead, now I have to do a Google Street View and virtually scout the location, with no results. All of the buildings except Dr. Stein's office appear to be vacant or changed. The landscape has shifted so much now that the hospital and Mount Union University have purchased so many large tracts of the surrounding area. I can only rely on the map in my head now. It's like being dropped somewhere new in a videogame and feeling out the lay of the land because the rest of the world is dark.

Next, I plug in anything I can remember into the search bar. The street name and the surrounding businesses and every variation of the words "vintage store in Alliance, Ohio." The results kind of jogs my memory, and I tell my sister with pride the store neither of us can remember was Marc's. Before it moved farther up State Street, that is. Maybe that location has been there so long this old building was starting to be scrubbed from our memories. But I am wrong. The actual store comes to me randomly one day after our call. The store was Bud's. A discount drug store similar to the one I'd mistaken it for. If I remember correctly, the mascot was a man in a striped vest and straw hat in the style of the chimney sweep from Mary Poppins. None of this is really important, but I couldn't get it out of my head. I *needed* to know this place. I *needed* to have it solid enough to touch to make sure it was at one time real.

• • • • •

A BRIEF HISTORY LESSON FROM the local library's website tries to pin down how my hometown got its name, but of everything I read one thing was the most noteworthy to me: Alliance is sometimes referred to as the town where Main Street is a dead end. This is because when the street was constructed it brought people from the train station into the heart of all of it. Maybe the platform just across the street from the Elks is the remnants of that hub. There's been an extension added to the street in recent years, but that just juts off into the distance like a broken arm. Locals know where Main Street truly begins and ends. I wrote an essay once about this nickname and sent it out into the world never thinking nearly a decade later I'd still be pining about where I was raised.

In Alliance, Ohio. In the shadow of the Football Hall of Fame (which I've only visited once because a partner from out of state wanted to see it) and the lingering jokes of toxic Cleveland. More recently we've been in the footprints of LeBron. In a town once built on the backs of steel mills and factories. Among the working-class families of the '80s and beyond. None of this is important in the grand scheme of things, but it points me to the fear. It harbors the worry that the longer I stay away the further and further I get from who I am, was, or could be.

I no longer worry about the "what if" of not leaving this place. I worry now about the "what if" of not returning. What I can, and will, miss by staying in a city such as Philadelphia that is as much my home as it is not. I come back to that essay I wrote and how I am still reconciling what I am missing. I am still trying to piece together the love and grief of this place. Trying to see beyond a veil of tears or drinks or nostalgia and see what really is.

● ● ● ● ●

There is something ruggedly beautiful about Ohio. These ramshackle houses dropping their roof shingles into the snow, sagging under the weight of closed steel mills and forgotten industry, are something that must be experienced. Growing up here, I never paid attention to anything other than the frayed edges of my hometown. I resented the gritty voiced pick-ups tooling down Main Street and the trickle of the fountain in Kidd Lake. All I wanted was to leave this tiny place behind and start a life somewhere big and rushing a mile a minute. But this place, now stuck in time, rather than losing a battle against it, now defines exactly who I am.

There is abandonment everywhere here. It is full of empty places once cared for and occupied. Here is where the lesson lies. It's what we do with the empty that defines us. It's what we fill those spaces with that either rebuilds us or destroys us. I've been rebuilt by home. And I could say it was the hands of my parents reaching out or the jolts of reality from my sister or the laughter of my best friend, but those are the final touches of the story. I've been restored by my connection to this place. I've filled the empty places here in order to remember exactly who I am.

There is a stretch of curve on the two lane street leading into town where the trains race the shoulder and light breaks through the trees. No matter where I've been, when this expanse of asphalt appears before me I know I am home. When I can smell the aluminum in the air and the wash of purple and white college flags ripple the air, I settle into myself. Here people know the empty that comes with the city limits and they do their best to fill it.

Some of us work to rebuild this square footage with barbershops and salons. Others want nothing more than to raise their children in the same parks and classrooms that have existed since before our grandparents. In these ways, we are recreating tradition, a nation of Blue Devils, Aviators, and Purple Raiders. The rest of us may complain of the confines of our home, yet we arrive each summer at the Carnation Festival and loft our children in the air to catch candy and beads. And we eat at the diners now hanging on by a thread and drive the same loop, cruising to be seen. It has been this way since high school and will be the same in our old age. We figure as long as we patrol these streets the emptiness will retreat. And we are right.

Because even as the potholes grow larger and the homes are left vacant, new things begin to fill the empty space beside them. Each time we think this town has died, there are signs of life. Be it the return of each of us individually or the mass gathering of a family reunion, we re-enter this space and fill it to brimming until the emptiness drives us out again. This is how it is, an ebbing and flowing, a rebuilding, a destroying until the dust settles and we are welcomed back. [17]

---

17 Athena Dixon, "Where Main Street Is a Dead End," *Pluck! The Journal of Affrilachian Arts and Culture*, no. 12 (2015).

Auld Lang Syne

The tears are nothing new. They appeared last year and most of those before, although the cause has shifted and changed each time. On the last night of 2018, I was standing on the Cherry Street Pier with Kym in the rain watching fireworks. My eyes were a bit watery because there is something about gathering in cheer with others that hits me in the heart. I hadn't minded the bodies bumping against mine—jostling to poke camera phones between the crowd to capture the hazy explosions in the sky.

This New Year's Eve I am drinking whiskey-spiked iced tea alone in my apartment. Just like the year before there is no one else here, no voice on the other end of the phone. The world has cracked open its doors, and across nations there are crowds of people gathering in numbers although they are still masked and, when possible, socially distanced. Instead of being among one of these crowds, cheering the incoming year, I am watching *Dick Clark's New Year's Rockin' Eve* when a wash of tears forms. When Ryan Seacrest proclaims we've made it to 2022, I ask of the image of him smiling on the television, "Have we?" before the first few tears fall.

This time I am crying because I am still here, and despite the absolute internal chaos of the last twelve months, this is a feat of which I am proud. I find the familiar in the beginning strains of "Auld Lang Syne," but there is scant time to feel the melancholy of the new year before the network swaps the burgeoning nostalgia for "Theme from New York, New York." I mute the television. I have a love-hate relationship with the city, but each year I find myself somehow treating it as the center of the world.

I cry for another sixty seconds before my phone begins to pulse with texts. When I open them, the electronic confetti of each of them explodes across the screen. It is indeed a happy new year if only for the reason we've survived two of these diseased years, but this week my aunt was claimed by COVID-19, and there is a sense of failure because my bloodline had been spared this ravage. Once the disease took hold, it seemed to spike through those I know, and I could only hope no more were left dead in its wake. That wouldn't be the case.

Those deaths, and this grief, is why I am alone tonight. In a city of over a million, even amid a global pandemic, there are plenty of places I could be just to feel a little less alone. Yet, it is easier to splash more liquor into my glass and swirl it to cool among the flower-shaped ice cubes as I make my way from the kitchen to the sofa. I plop onto the cushions and turn the volume up on the TV. I don't know who the performer dancing across the screen is, but I can gather up some of the energy, and it anchors me just below the surface of my growing sadness.

A few days ago, I sat at my desk and stuffed mementos into a metal tin shaped like a slice of bamboo. I called this my Intentions Jar and filled it with trinkets representing what I hoped for the coming year. A dollar and coins for prosperity.

Two lengths of Chanel ribbon for a bit of luxury. A pecan for things to grow. Strawberry candies for sweetness. Crystals and wood to ground me. A Book Nerd pin to remind me to keep writing. A note that I will read when New Year's rolls around again. In the past I'd spent the final night of the year reviewing the memories in my Good Things Jar—a collection spanning the joy of the prior twelve months. The jar for 2019 was the last one I'd completed. The toll of the years that followed was too much to memorialize much of anything. All of the years since are rolled into a single tin—a fraction of this prior joy. This, too, is grief.

Between the liquor and takeout I remind myself this sort of New Year's Eve is not unique in the world. There are so many like me—caught between isolation and the desire to be among a thick of people. There is a twinge of pain, too, when I realize the diminished likelihood I will ever spend a night like this in Times Square. I've always wanted to witness that magic—under a rain of falling paper and kissing someone at midnight like in a movie. All the practical knowledge of what it takes to stand in the cold for hours on end with a bladder bursting just to hold on to a few inches of pavement is easily pushed aside for the romanticism of it all. When I come back to my rational mind in the morning, I know this experience is nothing I actually want, but when there is no choice in the matter the desire to have what's just out of your grasp skyrockets.

· · · · ·

ON NEW YEAR'S DAY, when my phone rings and I see a photo of me and Angie filling the screen, I answer after a few rings. The last we'd spoken my aunt was still among the living and I'd been clinging to the idea that no change was for the best.

Angie offers her condolences before we launch into a conversation about the performance of grief. Of how we expect it to be grand. I liken it to a crater, and later in an Instagram post, I say sometimes it is like wind pushing you along the path. There are days you feel it and those you forget it even exists. Since my aunt has died I've been stuck. Not crying as I would expect. Not too ill to eat or sleep or function. Just stuck like I know the world has fundamentally changed and there is nothing I can do about it.

Angie and I settle into the idea that perhaps quiet grief, the kind I am feeling now, can turn into a performance—that we are trying our best to mimic how the largeness of a death is expected to be shown in order to convey we are actually connected to the loss. That we are feeling the pain and absence. The both of us understand, far too intimately, that grief is not always roaring. Sometimes it whispers so closely to your ear you are the only one who knows how cruel it can be. I know I should cry and scream, but my throat is hollow.

Angie asks me how I am faring, and I tell her I've checked out of the world. Purposefully, I've stopped switching on the news or reading current events. Sometime, in the bridge between 2020 and 2021, I lost the ability to juggle the daily need to survive this current life and remain informed. For months on end I streamed CNN on a loop each morning as I sat at my desk. I marveled at just how many bodies could pile up and knew that the piling was not stopping. I saw fires and protests and bullets, and at some point the hollowness in my throat started to choke me. I say to Angie that my life has moved from the macro to the micro. What matters to me are those in the intimate spaces closest to my heart. If I can ensure their safety, and keep a hand on each of them, I've done all I can do.

This is a performance of grief for the world just on a smaller scale. It is the grieving of time and closeness and intimacy with my family because the world in its current state demands the performance of isolation so all of us can survive. Where Angie and I settle toward the end of the conversation is that I've become much more accustomed to this new version of isolation. Before these last two years, I'd been proud to say I was able to be alone. *This* alone is not what I'd been living.

Isolation exists within the scope of grief. It took the dissection of these last years, and the life beyond it, to decide this was true. I've written before about how long it took to mourn my high school sweetheart and how I'd divorced myself from his absence so I could manage what it was like to truly feel he was gone. And what guilt came along with that grief—how I'd convinced myself that since our lives had untangled I was no longer permitted to feel such a big and unwieldy thing. That perhaps why I disconnect is because the tenderness I've always thought life would be borders too closely to pain and I don't know what to do with that. So I break the feelings down into smaller pieces I can handle. Chipping away at each one in silence until I can say it's all neatly put away. When my aunt passed I did this from a distance because it was the best tool I had. All of this shaping of grief, and its subsequent isolation, can manifest in hiding behind easy escapism or in the glow of a screen, or moving hundreds of miles away, but it's all spun out from the same emotions—fear, hurt, insecurity.

· · · · ·

ONE OF THE MEANINGS of *auld lang syne* is times long past. I try to work my mind around this concept. I keep circling how this relates to grief and performance and isolation. There are so many ways to make sense of this. A long time past life and suddenly we *are* in grief. We are echoing in the vastness of what could have been.

I land here late in January after Ryan Seacrest has long since faded from my screen. My fingers close around a slim envelope, addressed and stamped, that's fallen to the bottom of a pile of writing scraps. The name neatly in cursive in the center of the bright white pushes me back into the sofa. When I slide my fingertip beneath the sealed edge, I feel like I'm opening a time capsule. July looms as large as it had those months ago. What comes back is the pink mausoleum at the end of a long line of cars. A red rose pushed into my hands as a remembrance. A scattering of tissue scraps across my cheeks.

The card, written to my aunt upon the passing of her only child, is brief. I'd written in it that sometimes saying you are sorry isn't enough in the hugeness of death, but it is something. I say I love and miss her. Write the obligatory "if you need anything I am here." I close my condolences with an Avijeet Das quotation. "Life is all memories. People may not be present in body, but they are with us in spirit." When I find this card, it has been nearly a month since she too has passed, and it sends me into a sort of spiral. I've kept her online obituary open on my laptop the last few weeks, and after a quick misting of my eyes I allow myself to click the red *X* in the right-hand corner. I've been convinced closing this portal was a disrespect. I know now that it is not.

· · · · ·

TIMES LONG PAST. Well beyond when this card should have been sent. A long time across a turnpike and across the gulch of the virus that will kill her five months after it is written. This card is a heavy thing. It makes me rethink my self-imposed distance and whether or not it is time to return home. My lineage is aging, and even if I am not ready, I am now becoming an elder. It is terrifying. To face loss and age and absences that keep mounting no matter how hard I try to look away from them. The card brings guilt I know will never be assuaged because the only one who can tell me it is okay can't speak to me in ways I can hear.

I circle again to grief and isolation. How maybe for a few shining moments as one year comes to a close and another opens, we are all gathered in collected grief and joy. Chapters are ending and we are shaking off the bad more than the good. We think the flip of a calendar can change the path and right the world. We just need to find the right combination of promises to keep things on track the other 364 days. We look to each other, over rims of glasses and in washes of confetti, and sing whatever words of the song we know. Others of us listen from home for fireworks and gunshots, waiting for the phones in our hands to light with someone reaching into the new year with us. We grieve the illusions of the prior year and assign joy to things yet to happen.

I think, in some ways, my book has become about death. Death of ideas and dreams and plans and all the minutiae used to build a life. I believe, when I am true to my actual feelings and not putting on a brave face, that life is a series of tiny deaths. Morbid on the surface, sure, but that's not necessarily a bad thing.

One heartbreak, and the person you were before is gone. A singular triumph, and the moment preceding dies a death no one mourns. Each morning is the grief of the night before. It's what's in front of us—new life—where we should focus. But here, in the moment, none of that matters because my grief is thick. In just over a year, death has circled too closely to be ignored.

I find myself thinking "Auld Lang Syne" is much more a song of loss than it is of celebration. I watch the people on the screen hug and kiss, and I even watch a couple get engaged. This happens every year, to be honest, but the months since have wiped these memories from my brain and it all seems new. Beneath the fluttering confetti and bright lights, the fallen paper soaks up the footprints of those attending—all the dirt and vomit and grime that comes with people gathering.

A tiny army will swoop in after the square has been cleared and sweep away the tatters left behind. When the city fully wakes, what was left of 2021 will have been stuffed into bags and bins. This is, of course, all symbolic. What do we sing? *Should old acquaintance be forgot / And never brought to mind?* Yet each year we return, plugged into each other with hope and possibility hanging over our heads, waiting for the neat ending of time and a clean slate to begin again.

Acknowledgments

"Distillation" appears in *Shenandoah*, Volume 70, Issue 2, Spring 2021.

"Where Main Street Is a Dead End" appears in *Pluck! The Journal of Affrilachian Arts and Culture*, Issue 12, 2015.

A version of "You Have the Right to Remain Silent" appears in *Grub Street Literary Magazine*, Volume 70, 2021.

The core of this book is very much built around themes of loneliness, disconnection, and isolation. How they can create shadows in which to hide or shine so brightly all that you are is exposed. These feelings were amplified by the 2020 lockdowns and the uncertainty and fear they caused, but these emotions have existed in my life for as long as I can remember.

Yet, just as much as I've felt the weight of these feelings I've also felt the opposite. I am vastly loved and supported by a community of family and friends. Each of these people has helped carry me through the writing of this collection, and I offer every bit of love and gratitude I have to them along with so many others, including

My parents, Albert and Sharon Dixon

My sister, Evona Bowman, and my brother-in-law, Michael Bowman

Acknowledgments

Marisol Serrano and Kymberli Morrell

Jameel Roberts

Angie Chatman

My readers Cija Jefferson, Jeida Walker, Sawyer Lovett, Gabrielle Lawrence, Jen Soong, and Lara Lillibridge

The Zora's Den Writing Group

The HippoCamp Conference community

Every writer, editor, creative, and reader who beamed into my life via Zoom and social media in this whirlwind of a time

And a special thanks to Hanif Abdurraqib and the entire staff of Tin House for taking such care with my work.

Works Cited

Bronzilla. "7 People Found Dead Years After Their Death."
YouTube. July 18, 2015. https://www.youtube.com/
watch?v=rYRLWiJ6Bfs.

Brown, Ashley. "'Least Desirable'? How Racial Discrimination
Plays Out in Online Dating." NPR, Jan. 9, 2018. www.npr.org
/2018/01/09/575352051/least-desirable-how-racial-discrimination
-plays-out-in-online-dating.

"Doppelgänger." Wikipedia. Sept. 19, 2022. https://en.wikipedia
.org/wiki/Doppelg%C3%A4nger.

Duong, Kim. "Here's What 11/11 Means & Why Seeing 1111 Is Such
a Powerful Sign from the Universe." *StyleCaster*. Aug. 12, 2022.
https://stylecaster.com/feature/11-11-date-meaning-1063029/.

Gavagan, Rob. "10 Gruesome Bodies Discovered Years Later |
Twisted Tens #13." YouTube. Oct. 28, 2015. www.youtube.com
/watch?v=tRv98h6l49I.

Hammer, Josh. "The Dying of the Dead Sea." Smithsonian.com.
Oct. 1, 2005. www.smithsonianmag.com/science-nature
/the-dying-of-the-dead-sea-70079351/.

Howard, Sheena C., and Claudia Bucciferro. "The Symbolic, the Real, and the Ladies of Wakanda." In *Why Wakanda Matters: What Black Panther Reveals about Psychology, Identity, and Communication*, edited by Sheena C. Howard, 17–33. Dallas: BenBella Books, 2021.

Howitt, M. "The Spider and the Fly." Poetry By Heart. Retrieved March 6, 2023. https://www.poetrybyheart.org.uk /poems/the-spider-and-the-fly/.

Kleinfield, N. R. "The Lonely Death of George Bell." *New York Times*, Oct. 17, 2015. www.nytimes.com/2015/10/18/nyregion/ dying-alone-in-new-york-city.html.

Lam, Elisa. "Nouvelle-Nouveau." *Nouvelle/Nouveau*. https://nouvelle-nouveau.tumblr.com/.

Lewis, Helen. "What It's Like to Be a Leftover Woman." *Atlantic*, Mar. 12, 2020. https://www.theatlantic.com /international/archive/2020/03/leftover-women-china-israel -children-marriage/607768/.

Morel, Laura C. "Reclusive Woman May Have Been Dead in Largo Home for Three Years." *Tampa Bay Times*, Aug. 29, 2019. https://www.tampabay.com/news/publicsafety/body-found -inside-largo-home-identified/2136469.

Morley, Carol. "Joyce Carol Vincent: How Could This Young Woman Lie Dead and Undiscovered for Almost Three Years?" *Guardian*, Oct. 8, 2011. www.theguardian.com/film/2011/oct/09 /joyce-vincent-death-mystery-documentary.

Rooksby, Maki, Tadaaki Furuhashi, and Hamish J. McLeod. "Hikikomori: Understanding the People Who Choose to Live in Extreme Isolation." The Conversation, Sept. 13, 2022. https://theconversation.com/hikikomori-understanding-the -people-who-choose-to-live-in-extreme-isolation-148482.

Schwartzberg, Eric. "$1.6 Billion and Counting: Booze Sales Surging in Ohio During Pandemic." Dayton Daily News, Jan. 27, 2021. https://www.daytondailynews.com /news/pandemic-fueled-spirits-sales-surged-in-ohio-in -2020/QOSYRITYZZFQ7N5DHYNVALRNU4/.

Teo, Alan R., and Albert C. Gaw. "Hikikomori, a Japanese Culture-Bound Syndrome of Social Withdrawal? A Proposal for DSM-5." *Journal of Nervous and Mental Disease* (June 2010). www.ncbi.nlm.nih.gov/pmc/articles/PMC4912003/.

Athena Dixon is a poet, essayist, and editor. Her work is included in the anthology *The BreakBeat Poets Vol.2: Black Girl Magic* and her craft work appears in *Getting to the Truth: The Craft and Practice of Creative Nonfiction*. Athena is an alumna of VONA, Callaloo, and Tin House, and has received a prose fellowship from The Martha's Vineyard Institute of Creative Writing. Born and raised in northeastern Ohio, Athena now resides in Philadelphia, Pennsylvania.